Steinbeck and Film

UNGAR FILM LIBRARY

Stanley Hochman, *General Editor*

Steinbeck and Film

WITHDRAWN

Joseph R. Millichap

with halftone illustrations

FREDERICK UNGAR PUBLISHING CO.

New York

Copyright © 1983 by Frederick Ungar Publishing Co.
Printed in the United States of America

Library of Congress Cataloging in Publication Data

Millichap, Joseph B.
    Steinbeck and film.

      Bibliography: p.
      Filmography: p.
      Includes index.
      1. Steinbeck, John, 1902–1968—Film adaptations.
    2. Steinbeck, John, 1902–1968—Moving-picture plays.
    3. Moving-pictures and literature.   I. Title.
    PS3537.T3234Z745   1983   791.43′75   83-4949
    ISBN 0-8044-2630-9
    ISBN 0-8044-6500-2 (pbk.)

For Margaret Millichap, who helped with my first Steinbeck study, and for Paulette Millichap, who helped with this most recent one.

Contents

Acknowledgments

The critical attitudes evident here were influenced by a number of scholars; this debt is acknowledged more formally in the Selected Bibliography. In particular, the author is indebted to Warren French and Robert E. Morsberger. Other insights were provided in discussion with colleagues, students, and friends, especially Thomas Bohn, Dean of Communications at Ithaca College. Encouragement, editorial advice, and patience were provided by Stanley Hochman, editor of this series for Frederick Ungar Publishing Co. The University of Tulsa also afforded help in terms of grant support and typing assistance. Hazel Kight and Deretha McIntire typed the handwritten manuscript, no easy task. The author's wife, Paulette Millichap, also helped with both thoughtful discussion and practical support. All of this aid is gratefully acknowledged; without this generous assistance the present study would not exist.

Chronology

1902   John Ernest Steinbeck born in Salinas, California on February 29.

1919   Graduates from Salinas High School.

1920   Enrolls at Stanford University.

1924   Publishes two stories in the Stanford *Spectator*.

1925   Leaves Stanford permanently, without degree; visits New York City.

1929   *Cup of Gold.* (novel)

1930   Marries Carol Henning; meets Ed Ricketts

1932   *The Pastures of Heaven.* (novel)

1933   *To a God Unknown* (novel); "The Red Pony" in *North American Review.*

1934   "The Murder" wins O. Henry Award as best short story of the year.

1935   *Tortilla Flat* (novel) (Commonwealth Club of California Gold Medal).

1936   *In Dubious Battle* (novel) (Commonwealth Club of California Gold Medal); "The Harvest Gypsies" in San Francisco *News*; travels to Mexico.

1937   *Of Mice and Men* (novel and play—Drama Critics' Circle Award); chosen one of the outstanding young men of the year.

1938   *The Long Valley* (story collection); *Their Blood is Strong* (non-fiction).

1939   *The Grapes of Wrath* (novel, Pulitzer Prize); *Of Mice and Men* (film).

1940   Explores Gulf of California with Ed Ricketts; *The Grapes of Wrath* (film).

1941   *The Sea of Cortez* (non-fiction); *The Forgotten Village* (book and film).

1942   *Bombs Away!* (non-fiction); *The Moon is Down* (novel and play); divorces Carol Henning; *Tortilla Flat* (film).

1943   Marries Gwyn Conger; visits the European war zone for the New York *Herald Tribune*; *The Moon is Down* (film).

1944   *Lifeboat* (film); Son, Thomas, is born.

1945   *Cannery Row* (novel); "The Pearl of the World" story); *A Medal for Benny* (film); *The Red Pony* (as separate volume).

1946   Son, John, is born.

1947   *The Pearl* (novel and film); *The Wayward Bus* (novel); trip to Russia.

1948   *A Russian Journal* (non-fiction), with photographs by Robert Capa; divorces Gwyn Conger; Ed Ricketts dies in an automobile accident.

1949   *The Red Pony* (film).

1950   *Burning Bright* (novel and play); marries Elaine Scott.

1951   *The Log From the Sea of Cortez* (non-fiction), including "About Ed Ricketts."

1952   *East of Eden* (novel); *Viva Zapata!* (film).

1954   *Sweet Thursday* (novel).

1955   *Pipe Dream* (Richard Rodgers and Oscar Hammerstein II musical comedy based on *Sweet Thursday*); editorials for *Saturday Review: East of Eden* (film).

1957   *The Short Reign of Pippin IV* (novel); *The Wayward Bus* (film).

1958   *Once There Was a War* (non-fiction).

1960   Tours America with his dog Charley for three months.

1961   *The Winter of Our Discontent* (novel); *Flight* (film).

1962   *Travels With Charley* (non-fiction); receives Nobel Price for literature.

CHRONOLOGY

1964   Receives United States Medal for Freedom.

1966   *America and Americans* (non-fiction).

1968   Dies in New York City, December 20.

1973   *The Red Pony* (made for television film).

1976   *The Acts of King Arthur and His Noble Knights* (modern rendering of Malory).

1981   *East of Eden* and *Of Mice and Men* (made for television films).

1982   *Cannery Row* (film).

1

John Steinbeck and Film

The interrelationships of literature and film are many and complex. Literature has influenced film both as entertainment and as art, and in turn literature, both popular and serious, has been influenced by film. Unfortunately, these reciprocal influences have been appreciated little enough until quite recently.[1] Film critics have generally insisted on the unique qualities of their medium, while literary critics have often slighted film as a medium of escapist entertainment. Major modern writers have been read in connection with all sorts of esoteric matters, but the pervasive and profound influence of film has been relatively ignored. Even those literary artists quite obviously influenced by film have been neglected in terms of this important aspect of their work.

In spite of the fact that John Steinbeck has been significantly influenced by film, perhaps more than any other major American writer, there is still no satisfactory assessment of its importance to his literary achievement.[2] Steinbeck is the most often and the most successfully adapted of all our major writers, and he also wrote two original screenplays from which important films were made.[3] The best Steinbeck films demonstrate the qualities which made him a major writer: vital characters, strong narratives, real settings, significant themes, and a realistic style. The weaker Steinbeck films demonstrate, even define, his literary failings: an over-reliance on type characters, stock plots, cardboard settings, second-rate ideas, and a sentimental style.

This cinematic index proves even more significant in its historical pattern, one which parallels Steinbeck's literary career. The major critical question raised by Steinbeck's canon is why it declined so markedly after the critical and popular triumph of *The Grapes of Wrath* in 1939. Like his novels, the strong movie adaptations date from the 1930s; the films of the later decades show a sharp falling off. This historical development suggests that one cause of Steinbeck's literary achievement, as well as of his decline, is his relationship to film.

Significantly enough, Steinbeck's writing in the 1930s mirrors the documentary thrust of American culture during the Depression. In his best fiction he balances documentary realism and romantic allegory much like the great documentary photographers and filmmakers of the period.[4] For a variety of reasons, his later fiction was shaped more by the sentimental and meretricious example of Hollywood.[5]

Steinbeck's major development begins with *In Dubious Battle* (1936). His earlier works rested uneasily between a tired romanticism and an imitative modernism; even his first best seller, *Tortilla Flat* (1935) proved more a clever entertainment than a serious work of fiction.

In Dubious Battle concerns an agricultural strike in a California valley, and Steinbeck focuses on his material with realism and objectivity. The novel extends his earlier materials and themes, but its documentary stance contrasts with the often derivative, awkward, and sentimental postures of his previous books. The following year, 1937, Steinbeck published *Of Mice and Men*, a perfectly wrought naturalistic tragedy, which utilized his new objectivity in an action of smaller, more human, compass. Two itinerant agricultural workers dream of their own ranch, until their dreams are shattered by the harsh realities of their environment, both natural and social. A play version of the novel in 1938 further increased Steinbeck's popularity, while a short-story collection, *The Long Valley*, published the same year, advanced his critical reputation. Among its half-dozen fine pieces was his classic short novel, *The Red Pony,* which tells of a young boy's initiation into the adult world. Finally, in 1939, after several years of research and writing, Steinbeck published his greatest work, *The Grapes of Wrath.* This American epic on the theme of the Okie exodus to California won him a Pulitzer Prize and election to the National Academy of Arts and Letters. A best seller of the decade, it led in rapid order not only to a movie version but also to a screen adaptation *Of Mice and Men,* whose cinematic potential had previously been neglected by Hollywood.

A writer of great talent and imagination, during the late 1930s John Steinbeck entered into the mood of the country as few artists have ever done. The Depression had elicited a notable reevaluation of American culture, a reassessment of the American Dream. The 1930s vision balanced a harsh realism of observation with a warm emphasis on human dignity.[6] Literature and the other arts joined social, economic, and political thought in contrasting traditional American ideals with the bleak reality of breadlines and shantytowns. Perhaps the major symbol of dislocation was the Dust Bowl; the American garden became a wasteland from which its dispossessed farmers fled.[7] The arts focused on these harsh images and tried to find in them the human dimensions which promised a new beginning.

The proletarian novel, documentary photography, and the serious narrative film stemmed from similar impulses. Of course, the radical novel put more emphasis on the inhuman conditions of the dislocated, while the movies made more of the promising possibilities for a new day. The best balance was struck by documentary photographers and filmmakers: Dorothea Lange, Walker Evans, and Arthur Rothstein in photography; Pare Lorentz, Willard Van Dyke and Herbert Kline in film.[8] As a novelist, Steinbeck shared this documentary impulse, and it refined his art.

In the 1940s these delicate balances shifted both for the

culture and for John Steinbeck. The threats of totalitarianism
and war necessitated an affirmation of traditional values.
Realistic observation and objective analysis gave way to
sentimental propaganda. The change was again most obvious
on the movie screen, but there was a similar shift in American
literature. The fiction of John Steinbeck proved no exception.
The cultural milieu which had elicited his finest writing died
on the morning of December 7, 1941, when the Japanese
bombing of Pearl Harbor brought the United States into
World War II. Later, the anxieties of the Atomic Age and the
Cold War extended this new, simplified vision of America into
other decades. By the time the culture again changed direction, back to the concerns (and in some cases the styles) of the
1930s, John Steinbeck was too old to change back with it.

Steinbeck's major novel of the postwar period, *East of
Eden* (1952), is an attempt at another epic of the Salinas
country he had exploited in his early fiction. The book has its
moments, but as a whole it is surprisingly flat; it lacks
everything that made *The Grapes of Wrath* so moving. *East of
Eden* strives for universal generalizations by retelling the
Cain and Abel story, but it fails to establish the realistic
surface necessary to match its allegorical understructure.
Steinbeck's ideas are shallow and contradictory, his characters unmotivated and unbelievable, his plotting alternatively
obvious and rambling, his style prolix. In the postwar years
the overall decline of his talents was marked by these same
faults.

From an artist committed to wresting a realistic yet
humane literary vision from his native land, Steinbeck
evolved into a successful commercial writer, concerned with
making his materials both palatable and popular. The
changes in America after 1939 both reflected and occasioned
the changes in John Steinbeck himself. Many factors, some
universal, some personal were involved: the war, his divorces; the transformed literary scene, the death of his friend
and mentor, Ed Ricketts, the movement of America toward

Cold War conformity, and his move from California to New York. This study suggests an additional cause for his decline—his changing relationship to film.

A consideration of Steinbeck's films confirms a general pattern. The best adaptations—Lewis Milestone's *Of Mice and Men* (1939) and John Ford's *The Grapes of Wrath* (1940)—appeared at the high point of American cinematic realism in the years just prior to World War II.[9] The success of these film versions confirms the nature of Steinbeck's achievement in the original novels; it was no artistic accident that in both cases the original novels were formed by the same vision which was then shaping American film. In other words Steinbeck's best works translate smoothly to the screen because they are essentially filmic. Drawing their inspiration from the realistic tradition of documentary photography and film, they in turn provided inspiration for filmic works in the same mode. The documentary film Steinbeck scripted for Herbert Kline about a medical mission to Mexico, *The Forgotten Village* (1941), confirms this same element in his work.

It is significant that *The Forgotten Village* appeared directly before Pearl Harbor, and his next film, *Tortilla Flat*, directly after, in 1942. Victor Fleming's cleaned up version of Steinbeck's 1935 novel confirms the book's light mood. Further contrast with *The Forgotten Village* is provided by Irving Pichel's weak film adaptation of *The Moon Is Down* (1943). *Lifeboat* (1944), which Alfred Hitchcock directed from an unpublished Steinbeck short novel, is a preachy allegory which contrasts good Anglo-American allies and an evil Nazi interacting within the small compass of a symbolic craft adrift in a world at war. An unpublished story about the inhabitants of Tortilla Flat during wartime forms the basis of Irving Pichel's *A Medal For Benny* (1945), perhaps the weakest of the Steinbeck films. That same year the publication of *Cannery Row* emphasized that in his new fiction Steinbeck was beginning to imitate the film versions of his earlier books.

In the postwar period, Steinbeck wrote the screenplay of his short novel *The Pearl* (1947), a Mexican production directed by Emilio Fernandez. Like its source, the film was a reminder of his real talents, though it is less realized than the nearly perfect literary parable. Steinbeck also wrote a complete screenplay from *The Red Pony* for Lewis Milestone, who had so brilliantly directed *Of Mice and Men*. The 1949 movie is not as successful as the original short novel, as both author and director had faltered in their realistic visions after years of wartime propaganda. In the postwar period only Steinbeck's screenplay for Elia Kazan's *Viva Zapata!* (1952) suggests his old talent, and interestingly enough in mood and style the film recreated the movie biographies so popular in the 1930s. Kazan also directed the screen version of *East of Eden* (1955), somewhat strengthening Steinbeck's rambling epic by tightening it to a series of theatrical climaxes. However, this Hollywood epic is weakened by the same heavy symbolism that sinks the novel, as well as by overwrought performances and pretentious visual style. In directing *The Wayward Bus* (1957), intended as a vehicle for Jayne Mansfield, Victor Vicas did nothing at all to improve Steinbeck's dull pilgrimage. An honest if amateurish adaptation of an early Steinbeck story *Flight* (1961), scripted by Barnaby Conrad and directed by Louis Bisbo proved the last adaptation in Steinbeck's lifetime. Posthumous productions include television remakes of *The Red Pony* (1973), *East of Eden* (1981), *Of Mice and Men* (1981), and a multi-million dollar theatrical film of *Cannery Row* (1982). All of these works merely reiterate the critical successes or failures created by earlier films.

All in all, most of the postwar films to which his name is attached either as original author or screenwriter essentially demonstrate the same decline as Steinbeck's literary work: the movement from realism and commitment toward sentiment and popularity. They also suggest a source of this change in the productions of Hollywood itself. Steinbeck was no longer influenced by film as documentary, truthful and committed, but by movies as entertainment and escapism. The exceptions to this rule—notably *Viva Zapata!*—only help to prove it by utilizing the style of realism. Steinbeck had entered the enemy camp; in his later career he was writing not just with one eye on the movies, but with a vision literally made in Hollywood.

A consideration of John Steinbeck's relationship to film is essential to understanding the evolution of his career as a writer, as will be seen by the closer consideration of all the Steinbeck films. Naturally, the main emphasis will be on the most artistically important of them—*Of Mice and Men, The Grapes of Wrath,* and *Viva Zapata!*—but the others will be related to the central examples to demonstrate the development and decline of Steinbeck's career. The location of these films within the total context of Steinbeck's life and work demonstrates not only the importance of film in an overall consideration of his achievements, but in the development of modern American literature as well.

2

The Depression Decade

I. THE EARLY WORKS

Although he outlived the Depression by almost three decades, John Steinbeck remains a writer of the 1930s, perhaps *the* writer of the 1930s. His first novel, *Cup of Gold*, was published in 1929, the year of the Stock Market crash; ten years and six books later his finest novel, *The Grapes of Wrath* topped the bestseller lists for 1939. His epic of the Okies' California trek proved not only the culmination of Steinbeck's career, but of the decade itself; the novel and the film made from it remain perhaps the most representative artistic documents of the period. *The Grapes of Wrath* and Steinbeck's other writing during the Depression summed up the era for his own and later generations. The convergence of the spirit of the times with the mind of the writer was remarkable. From an awkward amateur, Steinbeck developed in a decade to the spokesman for a culture.

Steinbeck's background and development had prepared him for this role as literary spokesman. From early childhood, he wanted to be a story teller more than anything else. His biographer traces his literary ambition to his first reading of Thomas Malory's *Morte d'Arthur*, the most famous rendering of the legends of King Arthur and the Knights of the Round Table.[1] From the Arthurian legends, the King James Bible, Shakespeare, Milton and the other classics, Steinbeck derived a sense of high literary style and purpose. Great writing not only entertained with exciting tales, it illuminated the human condition by dramatizing the moral conflicts which beset humankind.

Of course, Steinbeck's first scribblings did not approach his models; rather he wrote imitative, amateurish pieces which displayed a vein of sophomoric satire. Yet Steinbeck, unlike so many would-be geniuses, kept writing—at Salinas High School, at Stanford University, and after, when he left without a degree to live as a "hippie" before that word had been invented. He sold an insignificant satirical piece in 1926, and this tiny success encouraged him to finish the book which would become *Cup of Gold.*[2] This first novel appeared the same year Thomas Wolfe's better known first novel, *Look Homeward, Angel* (1929). Steinbeck's book received none of the fanfare which greeted Wolfe's; it was in fact a flop. Perhaps this was just as well, for *Cup of Gold* was not the real Steinbeck. Though still readable, this fictionalized life of the pirate leader Henry Morgan is a curious hodgepodge of classic adventure and Lost Generation posturing.

Encouraged by its publication and initially supported by his parents—later by his young wife—Steinbeck plunged into an historical novel about the Salinas Valley. During this same period he worked on several books at once, even writing a murder mystery in nine days, which he then unsuccessfully offered for publication under the pen name "John Stone-brook."[3] In 1930, he married his first wife, Carol Henning, and he met his best friend and most influential mentor, Ed Ricketts. Carol provided encouragement and financial support for the budding writer, while Ed provided criticism and moral support. A marine biologist trained at the University of Chicago, Ricketts combined the objective attitude of a scientist with the wide sympathies of a humanist. The influence of his new friend led Steinbeck to a more objective viewpoint toward his materials, an emphasis on evidence and documentation. Ricketts convinced Steinbeck to modify his commitment to allegory and symbolism and to turn toward realism.[4]

His friend's suggestions moved Steinbeck to a new literary effort, a series of interrelated stories about a small fertile valley which he called the "Pastures of Heaven." It was to provide the title for Steinbeck's second published book in 1932. Although the book was another financial bust, it did bring Steinbeck much closer to his real subject matter and his true attitude toward it. *Pastures of Heaven* depicts the valley in the 20th Century, when its rich promise has been betrayed by the avarice and stupidity of its human inhabitants. The stories all turn on the disastrous effects of a group of newcomers, the Munroe family, on this idyllic setting. The book's major irony is that the Munroes are not pariahs or Faulknerian Snopses but only good, middle-class Americans. Steinbeck was beginning his life long assessment of the American Dream gone bad.

Also at Ricketts's suggestion, Steinbeck rewrote the historical saga of the Salinas Valley; in 1933 it was published as *To A God Unknown*—again with little reaction. Written for the most part before *Pastures of Heaven*, this novel occupies a place between it and *Cup of Gold*. Its subject is the history of the Salinas Valley, but it inclines toward the extravagant symbolic gestures and florid language of the first novel. The influence of D. H. Lawrence is easily discerned in its heavy mysticism and symbolism. For example, the story is climaxed by Joseph Wayne's ritual suicide. He cuts his wrists and lets his blood drain into the drought parched earth; almost immediately massive rain storms soak the valley. Yet the descriptions of nature and of Joseph's battle to build his ranch are taut and real, anticipating the better parts of *The Pastures of Heaven*.

The weakest element in *The Pastures of Heaven* is the tale of the little valley's two amiable prostitutes, Rosa and Maria Lopez. Though they are scorned by the valley's righteous hypocrites, Steinbeck is clearly on the side of these whores with hearts of gold, stock sentimental types who were to appear again and again in his books. The same story is also an early instance of Steinbeck's rather patronizing use of Chicanos as happy-go-lucky foils for the upright American middle class. In his next novel, Steinbeck combined his feeling for allegorical tale with fey ethnic humor; *Tortilla Flat*, published in 1935, is a series of interrelated stories about the *paisanos* of Monterey. The book is provided with an allegorical structure that parallels the adventures of a little band of hard drinking Chicano roughnecks with the stories of King Arthur's knights.[5] As a light diversion and literary entertainment, the book works well enough, so it soon became Steinbeck's first bestseller. The young writer made even more money from it when Hollywood bought the movie rights. It was his first property sold to the movies, though a film version would not appear until 1942. Steinbeck was now a maturing, modestly successful author with money enough to take his first trip to Mexico, later to become an important setting for his work.

More importantly, the success of *Tortilla Flat* provided the means for developing the more serious directions of his talents. Between his novels Steinbeck had written a number of fine short stories. Perhaps because of the discipline inherent in the form, these were tighter and more realistic pieces than his longer efforts. Most successful of these was the first version of *The Red Pony*, the story of a boy who matures with his experience of the death of his horse; it appeared in the *North American Review* in 1933. In the same year Steinbeck won the O. Henry Award for the Best Story of the Year for "The Murder," his tense account of a love triangle and its tragic conclusion. A comparable story is "The Raid," a harsh piece about two Communist labor organizers who are assaulted by a vigilante mob. Both "The Murder" and "The Raid" have the factual objectivity of good newspaper accounts; they center on sensational, violent events, but are written in a cool, detached tone that traces human motivation in moral delusions.

"The Raid" became one source for Steinbeck's first

artistically important novel, *In Dubious Battle* (1936). The novel tells the story of a violent agricultural strike in the "Torgas Valley" from the viewpoint of two Communist agitators closely resembling the pair in the earlier piece. Careful and objective in his handling of the material, the mature Steinbeck provided an almost factual case study of a strike. In a letter, he indicated that this was his conscious intention ". . . I had an idea that I was going to write the autobiography of a Communist. Then Miss McIntosh [his agent] suggested I reduce it to fiction. There lay the trouble. I had planned to write a journalistic account of a strike. But as I thought of it as fiction the thing got bigger and bigger . . . I have used a small strike in an orchard valley as the symbol of man's eternal, bitter warfare with himself."[6] Thus for the first time Steinbeck was able to combine his ambition to write great moral literature with his desire to chronicle his time and place.

Significantly, the novel takes its title from Milton's *Paradise Lost*, in which the phrase is used to describe the struggle between God and Satan; but it takes its subject from the newspapers and newsreels of the 1930s. The underlying structure demonstrates the universal struggle of good and evil, of human greed and selfishness versus human generosity and idealism. The protagonist, who is killed at the conclusion, is obviously a Christ figure, an individual who has sacrificed himself for the group. Here Steinbeck needs no overblown symbolic actions to support his theme. He lets his contemporary story tell itself realistically and in documentary fashion. In a letter he describes his method in the novel. "I wanted to be merely a recording consciousness, judging nothing, simply putting down the thing."[7] This objective, documentary, almost cinematic realism separates *In Dubious Battle* from his earlier fiction and announces the beginning of Steinbeck's major period. Unfortunately, *In Dubious Battle* never became a film, probably because it was too harsh for Hollywood at that time. Steinbeck's next novel, *Of Mice and Men*, would become his first film.

II. OF MICE AND MEN

In terms of faithful filmic adaptation, Lewis Milestone's *Of Mice and Men* is the best of the Steinbeck films. It almost perfectly translates the characters, plot, setting, style, theme, and meaning of Steinbeck's novel and play to the screen. John Ford's *The Grapes of Wrath* remains a more important film, a film of greater impact, but it fails to capture the power of Steinbeck's original, while Milestone's film proves at least the equal of Steinbeck's fictional and dramatic versions. Of course, the partial realization of *The Grapes of Wrath* as film can be explained by the greater size and scope of the novel. The smaller, tighter accomplishment of the short novel and play *Of Mice and Men* was easier to realize on the screen. The differences between the directors also must be considered. The better known of the two directors, Ford was a genuine *auteur*, a director who inevitably converted his source material into a vehicle for artistic vision. Such was at least partially the case with his version of *The Grapes of Wrath*, which was marked by John Ford's vision rather than John Steinbeck's.

Although Lewis Milestone is a fine director, he is not an *auteur*. His artistic goal was limited to recreating the literary vehicle on the screen. He has said of his work: "Throughout my career I've tried not so much to express a philosophy as to restate in filmic terms my agreement with whatever the author of a story I like is trying to say."[1] Milestone had followed this artistic program in directing his best films, especially *All Quiet on the Western Front* (1930), the classic war film drawn from the novel by Erich Maria Remarque. Other Milestone films of importance—all cinematic adaptations of plays or novels—include: *The Front Page* (1931), from the play by Ben Hecht and Charles MacArthur; *Rain* (1932), from the Somerset Maugham story; *A Walk In the Sun* (1945), from the novel by Harry Brown; and *The Red Pony* (1949), for which Steinbeck provided a screenplay based on his own story.

Milestone was a very successful adapter of literary works because in his films he recreated the style as well as the story of the original source. Born in Odessa, Russia, in 1895, he emigrated to the United States before World War I. After serving in the film branch of the Signal Corps, Milestone drifted to Hollywood where he swiftly progressed from film editor to director. His early silent films employ the style of German Expressionism, while his better known work in the sound era tends toward cinematic realism. He has said of this aspect of his work: "My approach, my style is governed by the story, not the story by my style."[2] Steinbeck's short novel and the play written from it appealed to Milestone for the very reason that most producers were afraid to tackle the work: its harsh realism. A complicated set of circumstances made it possible for him to create a work as artistically important as his earlier achievement in *All Quiet On the Western Front*.

Late in 1937, Milestone began filming for Hal Roach an adaptation of Eric Hatch's novel *Road Show* (1934), the story of a traveling carnival. After ten weeks of shooting the director was removed by Roach who argued that he was turning a comedy vehicle into a serious drama. Early in 1938, Milestone sued Roach for $90,000 in salary arrears, interest, and damages. Roach eventually settled out of court, offering to pay the production costs for a screen version of Steinbeck's *Of Mice and Men* in lieu of the disputed money. Thus Milestone's *Of Mice and Men* was almost completely a personal project, a labor of love. The director had read the book and seen the play, immediately concluding that the story would make an excellent film.[3] He had a screenplay written by Eugene Solow, and later he took it to Steinbeck for approval. Though he made a few minor changes, the novelist quickly approved of the project, the script, and the director.[4] Next, Milestone had to sweat out a session with the studio censors and the Hayes office, but again the changes were minor.[5]

Milestone was not only a fine artistic craftsman, but a very careful and canny businessman. Out of both artistic preference and budget constraint, he preferred to work with what were then comparative unknowns. Burgess Meredith, who had appeared on the Broadway stage was probably the best known member of the cast; his portrayal of George Milton adds a touch of stylized lyricism to the role. Lon Chaney, Jr., had played Lennie in a Los Angeles production of the play, and the role offered him a chance to escape monster roles. B-Western star Bob Steele was typecast as Curly, while Betty Field had her first important role as his wife, Mae. Stage actors Charles Bickford as Slim, Roman Bohnen as Candy, and Leigh Whipper as Crooks completed the cast and turned in uniformly excellent performances.

Milestone conferred on visual motifs with art director, Nicolai Remisoff, and with Steinbeck himself, who took the director to the ranch that had been the scene of the real action that had inspired the story.[6] Veteran cameraman Norbert Brodine competently filmed the piece, while Bert Jordan provided expert editing. The director was also much concerned with sound motifs, and he persuaded composer Aaron Copland to do a musical score which has since become a concert favorite.

In spite of this array of talent and a Best Picture nomination for the banner year of 1939 (when Victor Fleming's *Gone With the Wind* swept the Oscars), the movie failed at the box office. In desperation, United Artists even tried to sell it as a "sexploitation" picture; the posters featured Betty Field in seductive poses and said: "Unwanted, she fought for the one thing which is every woman's birthright."[7] Over the years, however, *Of Mice and Men* has been recognized as a Hollywood classic, and become a staple of film programs. As Steinbeck himself said, ". . . it is a beautiful job. Here Milestone has done a curious lyrical thing. It hangs together and is underplayed."[8]

Steinbeck's short novel and the dramatic version which he wrote from it present not only a lyrical vision of a friendship and a dream, but a harsh reality of the 1930s—the lives and deaths of little people disoriented and dispossessed by the conditions of the modern world. The book's accurate and dispassionate portrait of agricultural life in California during the Depression obviously prefigures Steinbeck's next novel, *The Grapes of Wrath*. Like that novel, *Of Mice and Men*, shows people reduced to an animal status by the pressures of the social world.

The characters, especially Lennie Small, seem almost primitive in their simplicity, but Steinbeck is careful to portray lives shaped by social as well as natural forces. Unable to control his impulses, simpleminded Lennie innocently commits a crime for which he is hunted to his death. Whatever leadership and order are found in the ranch world are provided by Slim, who keeps his passions strictly under control. George Milton exists somewhere between these poles, poetically dreaming of order and harmony on "a little place," while still succumbing to the easy pleasures of pool hall, barroom, and brothel. The behavior of these three men is motivated by the whole spectrum of human involvements, and social morality is as much a theme in *Of Mice and Men* as it was to be in *The Grapes of Wrath*.

Steinbeck's stylistic techniques are rooted in realism; the point-of-view is a restricted third person, and the tone as carefully distanced, dispassionate, and as impersonal as the camera lens:

> Evening of a hot day started the little wind to moving among the leaves. The shade climbed up the hills toward the top. On the sand banks the rabbits sat as quietly as little gray, sculptured stones. And then from the direction of the state highway came the sound of footsteps on crisp sycamore leaves. The rabbits hurried noiselessly for cover. A stilted heron labored up into the air and pounded down river. For a moment the place was lifeless, and then two men emerged from the path and came into the opening by the green pool.[9]

The novelist almost seems to be facilitating a film version of the book in his descriptive and documentary prose. Each chapter is introduced by a detailed report of the setting—a sort of establishing shot followed by several close-ups. Dialogue is simply recorded with no authorial directions. Steinbeck does not use overtly symbolic action to comment on his characters as he did in his earlier works.

Milestone's film version parallels Steinbeck's *Of Mice and Men* in its anti-omniscient viewpoint. His camera angles are nearly always at eye level, thus involving the viewer in a human way. The framing of shots, especially in the outdoor scenes, opens wide vistas of natural and social contexts for the immediate action. Composition is careful, detailed, and complex. The bunkhouse and barn interiors, for example, offer contextual details of social and animal life—pin-ups, bunks, harnesses. Long takes are used to capture George and Lennie's first conversation, while tracking shots connect the players' complex actions. Close-ups are deft, not heavily symbolic, and bits of montage editing emphasize action scenes such as Curly's confrontation with Slim, George and Lennie.

In perhaps the first use of a now common device, Milestone opens with a prologue before the credits. We are immediately thrust into the drama of real life rather than the details of Hollywood production. More importantly, the prologue sets the mood and tone of the film while establishing themes and motifs which will be continued throughout. Steinbeck preserves a greater dramatic unity by opening and closing his story at the narrow pool, but Milestone achieves greater dramatic force in translating George's remarks about the trouble at Weed into an exciting chase sequence. The prologue realistically extends the action of the narrative from the small world of the ranch to a larger world of Weed and the Salinas Valley country, and finally, by the implications of the hoboes on the train, to all of Depression-stricken California and America.

The opening shot establishes the balance between men and nature which will become thematically important. As the music rises dramatically, swirling stormy clouds darken the sky in a shot that recalls the opening of Pare Lorentz's *The River* (1937), an influential documentary film of the time.[10] After studying the sky, the camera looks down from eye level to examine a rabbit and a flock of quail. The inhabitants of this natural world feed peacefully until human legs intrude into the frame; then the camera pulls up to eye level to show George and Lennie running wildly. Several quick cuts between the pursuing posse and their quarry capture the excitement of the chase, while in the background the thunder rolls. Trapped like animals, the pair almost panic, until George leads them into an irrigation ditch. This immersion is accompanied by a cloudburst which evidently discourages the hunters, who have leaped across the ditch without discovering their prey. The emotional mood of the film (fear, frustration, hate), characterization (George as the leader, Lennie the follower), style (eye-level shots, careful framing in outdoor scenes), and theme (the relationship of human and animal worlds) are all established.

The next scene consists of one long panning shot which shows George and Lennie still running, now at night, to catch a moving freight train. When they climb into an open boxcar, George closes the door, over which the credits are then presented. After the credits, the train fades into the distance, and the next sequence is in the interior of a bus; the other passengers are scanned as the camera settles down for an extended take of George and Lennie in the front seat talking about their new jobs at the ranch. This sequence, added by Milestone, is drawn from a few retrospective remarks by George, and like the director's prologue it works to open up the context of the action.

The bus is full of ranch hands like George and Lennie, and the driver remembers having originally taken them to Weed. When George reacts angrily to the driver's prying, the pair are put off the bus and have to walk the rest of the way to the ranch. After several miles of hot pavement, George hurls a

George (Burgess Meredith) and Lennie (Lon Chaney, Jr.) hide from their pursuers in Lewis Milestone's *Of Mice and Men* (1939).

Jim Casey (John Carradine) and Tom Joad (Henry Fonda) have disarmed a deputy who invaded a migrant camp in John Ford's *The Grapes of Wrath* (1940).

Pilon (Spencer Tracy), Sweets (Hedy Lamarr), and Danny (John Garfield) in a tender moment from Victor Fleming's *Tortilla Flat* (1942).

A boatload of troubled allies under the guidance of the deceitful U-boat captain (Walter Slezak) in Alfred Hitchcock's *Lifeboat* (1944).

Kino (Pedro Armendariz), Juana (Marla Elena Marques), and their child during a tense pursuit in Emilio Fernandez's *The Pearl* (1947).

Tommy (Peter Miles) leads his cold and rain-soaked pony to the barn in Lewis Milestone's *The Red Pony* (1949).

Emiliano Zapata (Marlon Brando) astride his symbolic steed Blanco in Elia Kazan's *Viva Zapata!*

Cal Trask (James Dean) confronts his angry father Adam (Raymond Massey) in Elia Kazan's *East of Eden* (1955).

As Victor Vicas's *The Wayward Bus* (1957) bogs down, Ernest Horton (Dan Dailey) carries Camille Oaks (Jayne Mansfield) to safety.

"Buried Farm Machinery," Arthur Rothstein's now classic FSA photograph of Dust Bowl conditions in Oklahoma (1936) may have inspired descriptions in *The Grapes of Wrath* (1939).

Dorothea Lange's 1937 documentary photograph for the
Farm Security Administration was recreated in an early
sequence of Lewis Milestone's *Of Mice and Men* (1939).

Another Dorothea Lange FSA photograph recording the
misery of Depression farm families was cropped for the cover
of Steinbeck's *Their Blood Is Strong* (1938).

clod of earth at a signboard depicting a business man enjoying the comfort of an air-conditioned train, a life style in
sharp contrast to his own. The shot of George and Lennie
trudging down the dusty highway past the billboard seems
suggested by one of Dorothea Lange's documentary photographs for the Farm Security Administration.[10] In general, the
visual ambiance of Milestone's film, like that of John Ford's
later adaptation of *The Grapes of Wrath*, seems strongly
influenced by the documentary film and photography of the
1930s.

The next sequence presents Chapter One of the novel or
Act One, Scene One, of the play. George and Lennie stop to
rest beside a narrow pool of the Salinas River, and George
decides to spend the night there enjoying their last freedom
before their new job. Milestone's version stays very close to
the dialogue of the play, while his filmic style develops a
sense of intimate realism similar to the dramatic exchanges
of the stage. After filming the pair approaching from a slight
distance, the camera moves in like another person. Many of
the shots are held for long periods as both men are balanced
in the frame; the only cutting in the scene is from one speaker
to another. In fact, the editing becomes nearly invisible; it
does not, for example, close in on Lennie's dead bird (a mouse
in the novel) as a symbol, but only as a part of a developing
pattern of nature images within the context of the entire
Lennie-George relationship. Milestone does add one piece of
dialogue to the scene; the last thing George says before they
sleep is: "A man sure feels free when he ain't got a job . . . and
when he ain't hungry."

Their arrival at the ranch the next day proves the
wisdom of these words; the boss is angry because they have
missed a half-day's work. He soon makes it plain that working
on this ranch will be no picnic. In handling the interview with
the boss before the arrival at the bunkhouse, Milestone
reverses Steinbeck's order of events, though each event is
substantially reproduced. The greater complexities of social

life are mirrored in the increasing use of deep focus and in the greater detail of composition.

The scene opens as Candy, the aging bunkhouse swamper, leads George and Lennie across the ranch yard toward the boss's office. They are seen through the open window of the office and in the context of the cluttered desk and files. As they enter, the camera examines all the details of the interior which presents the complicated organization of the ranch as a business society. During the interview, Milestone's extended shots carefully compose the grouping of the four figures. Dramatic emphasis is provided by shifting the figures in front of the camera (the boss rises from his chair, Candy shuffles, Lennie cowers, George puffs himself up defensively) instead of by camera movement or cutting.

Steinbeck used a sort of verbal *mise-en-scène* in the depiction of the bunkhouse. Milestone picks up this cue and translates the picture of the bunkhouse perfectly to film. His camera is at eye level, inside the door, ready to follow the trio through the room and to locate them against all of the details Steinbeck mentions, adding a few, such as girlie pictures tacked to the walls. George's argument with Candy about bed bugs is neatly framed by two stacks of bunks and again done in an extended shot. In both novel and play Steinbeck brings the other characters, including the boss, into the bunkhouse for the interview. Milestone has the other characters presented outside, in the office, or against the natural backgrounds of ranch activity. Crooks, the black cripple who serves as stablebuck, limps by; Curly, the boss's son, rides up like a movie cowboy; Mae, Curly's wife, plays in the barn with her fleecy puppy; Slim, the muleskinner, drives by with his twelve-mule team. The director builds tension by inventing a fist fight between Curly and Whit, a young ranch hand, then moving to direct confrontations of Curly with Slim, George, and Lennie.

Milestone very carefully orchestrates these scenes in terms of composition and editing. Mountains, fields, and machinery are balanced to emphasize the movement of characters. Curly advances through the moving belts of the threshing machines; Mae peeks out from between the wagons at Slim; George has Lennie lift a wagon on his back in a demonstration of his superhuman strength. Deft montage editing depicts the various confrontations, and in the movements between each. Milestone draws back for distanced shots which locate the characters in the context of the ranch and the natural world. He holds the shots and lets the action play in front of the camera; farm wagons criss-cross in right-left, left-right lines of movement—a sort of folk ballet which gives a lively feeling to the natural life. Against this backdrop we see Lennie's brute strength, Mae's loneliness, and Curly's brutality; only Slim, the muleskinner and, to some extent, his new friend, George, know how to harness nature in an orderly way.

Instead of showing George and Slim talking in the bunkhouse, the director has them hold their conversation while riding in, washing up, and eating dinner. These scenes allow Milestone to do some nice composition with visual elements like the sinewy bodies of the ranchhands in the outdoor washhouse and the heaping piles of plain food on the tables of the cookshack. He also interpolates a contrasting dinner scene at the ranchhouse, where the boss and Curly wolf down their food as Mae simmers in silence. Finally she asks Curly to take her to the movies, but he saunters out saying that he has seen the picture with the "boys." Mae is left behind with her indifferent father-in-law and the antagonistic Chinese cook.

In contrast, the dinner conversation in the cookshack is voluble and pleasant, and the friendliness continues in a game of horseshoes during the early evening. The men of the bunkhouse, for all their disparate qualities, form a family more cohesive than the real family of the ranchhouse. The long sequence which forms Chapter Three of the novel and Act Two, Scene Two of the play, the shooting of Candy's dog, demonstrates this human solidarity. Carlson, a seasoned ranchhand who seems second in command to Slim, has been after Candy to get rid of his old sheepdog because it smells up the bunkhouse. The men commiserate with Candy, as all have dogs of their own, but finally they agree that he would do better to shoot the old dog and take a pup from the litter Slim's bitch has just dropped. Carlson volunteers to shoot the dog with his pistol.

Milestone handles this potentially melodramatic scene with a fine restraint, using the realism of the camera to limit the sentiment inherent in the subject. The scene unfolds within the earlier established bunkhouse decor, playing itself out in extended shots of the whole group debating the fate of Candy's dog. Many of these shots are angled through the bunks or other pieces of furniture, giving a fuller human context to the drama pictured. Only when Candy hears Carlson's shot does the camera close up on him isolated in his bunk. The scene requires this extended treatment because it prefigures Lennie's death at the conclusion of the film and suggests the essential fate of Candy himself.

Lennie is not present in the bunkhouse; rather he is out in the barn playing with the pup Slim has given him. Milestone crosscuts back to the ranchhouse to show Mae alone, pacing and brooding. She then decides to visit her puppy in the barn. Slim and Crooks have also headed to the barn to look after the mules, and she takes the opportunity to talk to Slim about why he absolutely rejects her (another scene invented by Milestone). But Curly, who is always checking on her movements, uses their proximity and the gift of the puppy to cause another confrontation. The resulting fracas leaves George and Lennie together in the bunkhouse, where they can discuss their plans.

They are not alone, however, for Candy is still quietly curled up in his bunk. When George begins another poetic description of their "little place," the camera holds on him and Lennie for a full five minutes; slowly, in the far background shadows, Candy changes his position as he hears their plans for the "little place." Then he gets up and crosses the room, filling the opening between George and Lennie. Hesitantly, he asks to be included in their plans. As he tells George that otherwise he faces only the county home, the camera moves to a close-up of his broken face. Candy had $340 to contribute toward the purchase of such a "little place." George climbs into his upper bunk to think the proposition over; the camera now looks over his shoulder down at the expectant Lennie and the hopeful Candy. Suddenly George jumps down; they will do it. They almost dance between the stacks of bunks, while the camera holds on all three yelling out their contributions and desires. Overall, the whole sequence is a splendid example of how cinematic style can evoke the full power of dramatic performances.

The next sequence, Lennie's fight with Curly, begins with extended shots of the group returning to the bunkhouse; Slim verbally puts down Curly, and then Carlson does the same. In his frustration Curly turns on Lennie, and Milestone uses his quickest cutting and most dramatic montage effects to achieve the sense of physical urgency the scene requires. The cuts jump from one fighter to the other, and to the circle of ranchhands urging Lennie to defend himself. Finally the badgered giant catches one of Curly's fists in his big paw and slowly crushes it. The camera holds on a tight close-up of the hands. Fortunately, Slim is able to browbeat Curly into covering up the fight, and Lennie is able to keep his job.

Milestone interpolates the next scene—Saturday night in the town barroom—which not only gives him the opportunity for another realistic composition, but again extends the contexts of the central narrative. George, though tempted by booze and floozies, limits himself to one beer, and leaves to mail a money order as a down payment on the little farm. Almost the whole sequence is shot from directly beside the booth where George, Whit, and Carlson sit with three good-time girls. This also allows Milestone to re-emphasize one motif, the tawdry dreams of Hollywood; the girls introduce themselves as Marlene Dietrich, Jean Harlow, and Greta Garbo; "Garbo" even camps, "I vant to be alone."

Greta Garbo's publicity-oriented aloofness exists in direct contrast with the real loneliness of Steinbeck's characters. One of the most lonely, Crooks, the black stablebuck, is featured in the next sequence. Lennie, finally tiring of his pup, visits his room in the barn. At first Crooks refuses to let him in, because he is refused admittance to the segregated bunkhouse. But Lennie's innocence encourages Crooks' trust, and this human contact opens him up to Candy as well. Soon Crooks is also in on the "little place" plan, and when George returns from town all three are drinking, smoking, and singing. Crooks' room, actually the harness room of the ranch, gives Milestone another carefully detailed setting that has symbolic overtones. As Crooks himself says, he has his own room, but also his own dung heap. The whole sequence is shot much in the same style as the bunkhouse scenes, and when Mae intrudes once more, Milestone has another opportunity to choreograph the movement of his figures before the camera.

The boss finds Mae with the men and tells Curly when he returns from town; Curly, unable to start a fight because of his hand, turns on Mae and throws her out the next morning. Milestone adds this scene between Mae and Curly, and it works very well in terms of motivating Mae's subsequent behavior toward Lennie. When she goes to the barn to retrieve her pet, she finds Lennie mourning over his puppy, the pup having gone the way of the mice and birds innocently crushed in his strong hands. Mae needs any sort of human response, and she begins to flirt with Lennie.

Steinbeck sets the barn scene's naturalistic implications; Milestone cinematically realizes them by photographing against this realistic backdrop and by viewing his characters through the perspectives of rails, pens, and hay bales. As Lennie and Mae talk, the camera does more close-up work than it has throughout the film. Each character is locked in a sentimental dreamworld—Lennie's of the "little place," Mae's of Hollywood. The unintended murder is handled deftly and with considerable decorum. Quick cutting captures the physical tension of the scene; and the camera holds a long close-up on Mae's shoes suspended a few inches above the ground by Lennie's iron grasp on her throat. Her left shoe dangles, then drops off, and a few seconds later Lennie lets her crumple to the barn floor.

Until the discovery of her death, life goes on much as usual. After Lennie runs, Slim's bitch comes back to her pups; Candy comes in and picks one out to be his; George and Crooks play at horseshoes. Candy and George discover Mae's body after the dog comes to them carrying her shoe in its mouth. With Slim's approval, George determines to kill Lennie himself, and so spare his friend the lynch mob organized by Curly. This final sequence is reminiscent of the prologue and the first scene at the narrow pool in both action and treatment.

George and Slim race to the pool where Lennie had previously agreed to hide if he got into trouble. Slim walks off as Milestone crosscuts to the posse led by the Sheriff and to the mob led by Curly. The camera holds extended takes of George and Lennie as George delivers his traditional monologue about the "little place;" now as George spins out the description, he has Lennie look across the narrow pool and imagine what it will be like. In a final act of human imagination Lennie does see the future that George so movingly pictures in poetic words. The camera holds them together for several minutes and then follows George as he pulls back and takes the pistol, a symbol of harsh reality, from beneath his jacket. Like Carlson he is a careful shot; he fires once, and turns his head in horror at his act. Milestone has Lennie fall into the pool, once again immersing himself as he had in the prologue.

The director also adds an epilogue in which Slim joins

George, an act of supportive comradeship, and George, at Slim's urging, surrenders the gun to the sheriff who has arrived with the posse. Then, after they have walked off, Copland's theme music rises and a final pull-back shot holds on the same scene as the seasons change—leaves fall and a squirrel scampers on the fallen tree where Lennie sat. Recalling the rabbit and quail of the prologue, the natural movement poetically suggests that Lennie has returned to the nature which he loved, leaving George to the greater complexities of society and social organization.

The excellent cast, the creative technical staff, and the director's thoughtful combination of their efforts into an extension of the novel, all make Milestone's version as powerful as Steinbeck's in its convergence of lyrical and realistic fictional and cinematic styles.[11] Of course, Milestone's filmic success was occasioned by Steinbeck's original novel, a work in turn created from the documentary vision of the photographs and films which chronicled America in the Depression decade.

III. THE GRAPES OF WRATH

Lewis Milestone's *Of Mice and Men* is the most faithful and perhaps the most artistically successful of the Steinbeck films, but John Ford's adaptation of *The Grapes of Wrath* (1940) is the most popular and the most important. Although Ford condenses, changes, and perhaps even distorts Steinbeck's greatest novel, his film is possessed of considerable artistic power and has been of wide social influence. Like the novel, the film became the source of the most pervasive and powerful images of 1930s America. Critics studying it have most often stressed the differences between novel and film, but the present study will emphasize the points of connection between them, especially the documentary heritage they both share.[1] However, though Steinbeck and Ford both absorbed the documentary tradition, the two artists differ fundamentally in the use they make of it in two great, yet different versions of *The Grapes of Wrath*.

Responding to a variety of social and artistic influences, Steinbeck's writing had evolved toward documentary realism throughout the 1930s. In fiction, this development is especially clear in *In Dubious Battle* (1936), *Of Mice and Men* (1937), and *The Long Valley* (1938). Even more obvious was the movement of his nonfiction toward a committed documentation of the social ills plaguing America during the Depression decade. Steinbeck's newspaper and magazine writings were detailed accounts of social problems, paticularly the plight of migrant agricultural workers in California's fertile valleys. The culmination of this development was *Their Blood Is Strong* (1938), a compilation of reports originally written for the *San Francisco News* and now published with additional text by Steinbeck and photographs by Dorothea Lange originally made for the Farm Security Administration. *The Grapes of Wrath* is the fusion of these developments in Steinbeck's fiction and nonfiction.

In his development Steinbeck reflected a general trend of American culture during the 1930s.[2] The failure of our social and economic institutions with the resulting human deprivation and misery cried out for careful documentation for which still photography, motion pictures, sound recording, and radio provided the instrumentation in various combinations during the 1930s. The first sound film had appeared as recently as 1927, and its resources, both social and artistic, had hardly been tried when the Depression began. President Franklin D. Roosevelt's New Deal made documentation into a national policy: first, to prove that the problems of the Depression really existed; second, to demonstrate that solutions to these problems could be found. Roosevelt himself mastered the new technology in his radio broadcast "fireside chats," which reassured a nervous nation. His administration created an alphabet soup of federal agencies all employing new technology to meet new social needs.

Almost immediately these powerful influences of social

necessity and technological innovation began to reshape other cultural institutions. The traditional social sciences, humanities, and arts were soon transformed by the realistic examples discovered in the new technologies. For example, all the social sciences felt a new thrust to document the common man's experience not just by statistical reports but through the use of letters, diaries, individual case histories, participant narratives, and photographs. The traditional arts also felt this urge toward photographic reality. James Agee expressed the importance of the filmic experience to the culture. ". . . the camera can do what nothing else in the world can do . . . perceive, record, and communicate, in full unaltered power, the peculiar kinds of poetic vitality which blaze in every real thing and which are in a great degree lost to every other kind of art."[3]

The other arts, often under the sponsorship of government agencies, strained after this poetic vitality in common life and everyday reality. Painting imitated photography, particularly in the style which decorated public buildings across the land and which became known as "WPA realism." Theater, dance, even music stepped toward the immediate sense of reality, especially in the works of Clifford Odets, Martha Graham, and Aaron Copeland. Fiction approached sociology in the works of Theodore Dreiser, James T. Farrell, and John Dos Passos. Perhaps the most representative development was the documentary book, a combination of factual reportage and documentary photography. The best known examples include the various WPA Guidebooks, as well as Erskine Caldwell and Margaret Bourke-White's *You Have Seen Their Faces* (1937), Archibald MacLeish's *Land of the Free* (1938) (with photos by Dorothea Lange and others), Dorothea Lange and Paul Taylor's *An American Exodus: A Record of Human Erosion* (1939), and James Agee and Walker Evans's *Let Us Now Praise Famous Men* (1941).

It is significant that Steinbeck first conceived of *The Grapes of Wrath* as just such a documentary book. In March

1938, Steinbeck went into the California valleys with a *Life* magazine photographer to make a record of the harsh conditions in the migrant camps.[4] Evidence indicates that he intended a documentary book on the model of *You Have Seen Their Faces.*[5] The reality he encountered seemed too significant for nonfiction, however, and Steinbeck began to reshape this material as a novel.

Although his first tentative attempts at fictionalizing the situation in the agricultural valleys involved irony and satire, as indicated by the early title *L'Affaire Lettuceberg,* Steinbeck soon realized that the Okie migration was the stuff of an American epic.[6] Reworking his material, adding to it by research in government agency files and by more journeys into the camps and along the migrant routes, Steinbeck evolved his vision.[7] A grand design emerged; he would follow one family from the Oklahoma Dust Bowl to California. Perhaps this methodology was suggested by the case-history sociology works of the day, perhaps by the haunted faces of individual families which stared back at him from photos as he researched in Farm Security Administration files.[8]

In discussing his plans for his later documentary film, *The Forgotten Village* (1941), Steinbeck remarked that most documentaries concerned large groups of people but that audiences could identify better with individuals. In *The Grapes of Wrath* he made one family representative of general conditions. The larger groups and problems he treated in short interchapters which generalized the issues particularized in the Joads. Perhaps the grand themes of change and movement were suggested by the documentary films of Pare Lorentz (later a personal friend), *The Plow That Broke the Plains* (1936) and *The River* (1937), with their panoramic geographical and historical visions.

Drawing on an archetypal theme from Malory, Bunyan, Milton, and the Bible—the ultimate source of his pervasive religious symbolism—Steinbeck transformed the journey of the Joads into an allegorical pilgrimage as well as a desperate race along U.S. Route 66. Just as he had made one valley symbolic "of man's eternal bitter warfare with himself" in his earlier novel *In Dubious Battle*, here one human journey becomes symbolic of the tragic history of the race. In addition, the book is an American exodus, an epic of the "Westering" experience of our culture. Its plot suggests not just the wagon train Western, but such classic novels as *Moby Dick* and *Huckleberry Finn*, which are shaped by symbolic expeditions into the American heart of darkness. Starting with an impulse to document the immediate reality of America in the Depression years, he began to mold his material to the timeless patterns of human experience.

He was not unique in this combination of intentions. The documentarians of the 1930s were among the decade's best artists. The documentary was perceived not simply as the factual presentation of evidence, but as "the creative treatment of actuality," as John Grierson, the pioneer of British documentary, defined the mode in the early 1930s.[9] Pare Lorentz had found an example for his filmic documentaries in the writings of Walt Whitman. The photographers of the period drew on the examples of the great graphic artists and painters. Dorothea Lange, for example, recreated a madonna pose in her striking cover for *Their Blood Is Strong* (1938). Dust Bowl painter Alexander Hogue also showed the despoliation of the virgin land as "Mother Earth Laid Bare," an allegorical figure of a wasted female frame revealed in the erosion patterns of an overworked farm.[10] Dramatists, dancers, and musicians used both classical and folk themes. The most significant artists of the 1930s struck an aesthetic balance between documentary realism and traditional symbolism to convey both their harsh social analysis and their affirmation of human dignity and purpose.

The Grapes of Wrath, both as novel and as film, are perfect examples of these complex tendencies, and they consequently became major cultural events. The novel was a sensational best seller from the very beginning. Published to generally fine reviews in March 1939, it was selling at the rate of over 2,500 copies a day two months later. Controversy helped spur sales.

As a semi-documentary its factual basis was subject to close scrutiny, and many critics challenged Steinbeck's material. Oklahomans resented the presentation of the Joads as typical of the state (many still do), while Californians disapproved of the depiction of their state's leading industry. The book was attacked, banned, burned—but everywhere it was read. Even in the migrant camps, it was considered an accurate picture of the conditions experienced there. Some 430,000 copies were sold in a year, and in 1940 the novel received the Pulitzer Prize and the Award of the American Booksellers Association (later the National Book Award).

Naturally all this excitement attracted the attention of Hollywood in spite of the fact that the controversy over the novel seemed to preclude a film version, or at least a faithful film version. *Gone With the Wind* (1936), the decade's other sensational bestseller, had presented the vision of America that Hollywood was most comfortable with, and the ethos of the film community was found in the 1939 movie version. Hollywood had its social conscience, however, and earlier in the decade it had produced such notable "social problem films" as Mervyn LeRoy's *I Was A Fugitive From a Chain Gang* (1933), King Vidor's *Our Daily Bread* (1934), Michael Curtiz's *Black Fury* (1935), Archie Mayo's *Black Legion* (1937), and, of course, Lewis Milestone's *Of Mice and Men* (1939). Even though such hard hitting, realistic films punctuated the flow of escapist fare made in this period, there was some surprise when producer Darryl Zanuck, associated more with musicals and gangster epics than with topical realism and literate adaptations, bought the screen rights to *The Grapes of Wrath* for $75,000—a respectable sum in that day. Zanuck, particularly in association with director Elia Kazan, was to confirm this shift in interest with postwar social films such as *Gentleman's Agreement* (1947) and *Pinky* (1949).

Committed to a faithful adaptation of Steinbeck's novel, Zanuck gathered a team of top professionals in order to insure the picture's success. For direction, he turned to John Ford, perhaps the only studio director, other than Lewis Milestone, capable of doing justice to the work.[11]

Born Sean O'Feeney to Irish immigrant parents in 1895, Ford followed his older brother Francis to Hollywood in 1914. After a stint as an actor (his credits include D. W. Griffith's *The Birth of a Nation*, 1915), he graduated to direction in 1917. His first efforts were two-reel Westerns featuring the legendary Harry Carey, but he soon was directing features, including *The Iron Horse* (1925), an epic Western focusing on the construction of the transcontinental railroad. Ford easily made the transition to "talkies" which derailed many other directors. In the 1930s he began a series of American melodramas (several starring Will Rogers, Oklahoma's favorite son) punctuated by two serious literary adaptations: Liam O'Flaherty's novel, *The Informers* (1935) and Sean O'Casey's play, *The Plough and Stars* (1936), both stories of the Irish rebellion of 1922. 1939 was a banner year for Ford. He revived the Western genre, in decline since the introduction of sound, with his classic *Stagecoach* (which also brought stardom to John Wayne), and he demonstrated his mastery of Americana with *Young Mr. Lincoln* and *Drums Along the Mohawk*, both starring Henry Fonda. All in all, he had given evidence of an artistic sensibility and a social conscience that clearly qualified him to be the director of *The Grapes of Wrath*.

However, Ford's strengths as a director, his qualities as an *auteur*, worked against the ultimate artistic realization of his Steinbeck adaptation. Although a man of some liberal (or at least Populist) sentiments (witness his treatment of the Irish Rebellion), Ford was fundamentally a conservative personality, as his postwar films indicate ever more clearly. His work is marked by a strained nostalgia for lost promise, rather than anticipation of a paradise to be regained. Thus he inevitably emphasized one element of Steinbeck's novel: the nostalgia for the simple life of the yeoman farmers's family lost in the mechanical complexities of the modern world.

In his conservative vision, Ford found one consistent institution of value in the changing world—the family. His concern for family life gave him a real sympathy for the Joads (he connected them with the dispossessed Irish peasants of the nineteenth-century famine), but his picture of them emphasizes the pathos of the family's disintegration and even implies that the family may be reunited. This feeling of loss is present in Steinbeck's original, but it is balanced by the development of a communal family, a sense of universal relationships. Ford misses this, much as he neglects the documentary interchapters and the topical social themes which form the surface of the Steinbeck work. While he was the perfect director to translate certain aspects of Steinbeck's novel—the epic journey in all of its allegorical significance, its nostalgia for a way of life gone by, and its picture of a strong family fighting disintegration—other aspects such as the social problems, the vision of social solutions, and the documentary mode were less fully realized.

Steinbeck's novel is successful precisely because it achieves a balance between the documentary and allegorical elements that reflected the influence of 1930s culture on his work. Ford's work in the 1930s also shows a developing sense of realism, but he retained a predilection for the epic and for melodrama. In spite of the attention to historically realistic detail that characterizes *Stagecoach*, that fine movie can be seen as essentially a Western romance when contrasted with *Young Mr. Lincoln*, a film Ford insisted was great because "everything in the picture was true."[12]

Ford's *The Grapes of Wrath* derives from many of the same documentary film sources as Steinbeck's novel. Pare Lorentz's classic film documentaries clearly influenced the outdoor scenes. Dorothea Lange and the other Farm Security Administration photographers provided the images of rattle-trap automobiles, the ramshackle Hoovervilles with their ragged inhabitants. Since the major scenes were studio shot, the film presents a somewhat glossier version of reality than the novel, but as is true of the film *Of Mice and Men,* the transitions from location to studio shots are much less noticeable to the untrained eye than in most films of the era. (Another source for the film's visual images may have been Thomas Hart Benton's illustrations for the Limited Editions Club edition of the novel, many of which Ford's frames closely resemble.)

In general, though the documentary thrust of the 1930s influenced both the film and the novel, Ford's version weakens this element in order to realize the universal story. When a frontier newspaper editor in Ford's *The Man Who Shot Liberty Valence* (1962) is asked whether he will publish the truth or the legend about the title character, he answers without hesitation. "Print the legend!" No one has more effectively printed the legend of America in film than John Ford. Yet the creation of legends has often obscured facts, the reality which must be the basis for the creative thrust of documentary.

Despite the fact that as an *auteur* Ford was the shaping intelligence of his films, since cinema is a collaborative art, he could never be the creator of the film in the same sense that Steinbeck is the author of his novel. *The Grapes of Wrath* had a remarkable production team, and its members inevitably left their mark on the final version of the film. The screenwriter, a sort of creative middleman between Steinbeck and Ford, was Nunnally Johnson. Though a competent craftsman, Johnson—who was also to script *The Moon Is Down* (1943)— has left no other scripts of lasting importance. He was a writer whose essential commitment was to the creation of successful Hollywood properties, and his screenplay for *The Grapes of Wrath* follows his pattern as already established.

As called for in the contract with Steinbeck, Johnson and Zanuck (who as a former screenwriter often worked on the scripts of films he produced) wrote a screenplay which is faithful to the letter if not the spirit of its original. In their script the linear story of the Joad's journey is preserved with some justifiable excisions. (In the opinion of some critics, *The Grapes of Wrath* might well have profited from pruning, especially in the initial chapters.) However, the screenplay tends to ignore the universal interchapters. Though some of this material is indeed transposed to the Joad story, such transposition alters the meaning of the events documented.

Other changes were dictated by the production code of the day, and though these can be lived with, the scrapping of the book's powerful final scene is certainly unfortunate. In the novel, the Joad daughter Rosasharn (or Rose of Sharon) has miscarried; later when the family encounters an old man weak from starvation, the young woman nourishes him at her breast. Some literary critics complained of the scene's sentimentality and heavy symbolism; nevertheless, her act movingly conveys the sense of the universal family which Steinbeck used to replace the disintegrating nuclear family. Though in 1940 a film could not have graphically presented this scene, it could easily have been suggested.

John Ford extended certain of the tendencies he found in the screenplay by grafting to the work his personal vision of the family, a vision realized with the aid of cinematographer Greg Toland. Unlike Johnson, Toland was more than just a competent Hollywood craftsman; he was a brilliant photographic artist, perhaps the best produced by the studio system. In fact, Toland was often a sort of co-author of the cinematic works he filmed for Hollywood's best directors. His work on *Wuthering Heights* (1939) for William Wyler, *Citizen Kane* (1941) for Orson Welles, and *The Best Years of Our Lives* (1946), again for William Wyler, provides good examples.

Toland's great talent was the imaginative use of photographic technique to solve literary problems in cinematic terms. (Many of the bravura visual effects in *Citizen Kane* are apparently Toland's rather than Welles's ideas.) Though he was to create many memorable moments in *The Grapes of*

Wrath, his contribution also tended to strengthen the pre-dominance of Ford's vision over Steinbeck's. Toland was essentially an expressistic rather than a realistic cinematog-rapher. In spite of documentary moments like the "March of Time" sequence in *Citizen Kane* or the airplane junkyard scene in *The Best Years of Our Lives*, the basic thrust of his work was toward the dramatic, the symbolic, and finally the romantic. Even his use of deep focus, ordinarily a realistic technique because it includes more of the whole scene, is always turned toward symbolic purposes, as in the scenes of the younger Kane with his sled in *Citizen Kane*. In *The Grapes of Wrath* his use of available light photography at first seems realistic, certainly more so than the glossy backlighting of the studio sets. Yet he so overdoes this device that the night scenes at the abandoned Joad farm seem almost Mannerist in style. Calling attention to themselves as pieces of art photog-raphy, they fail to present the subject realistically, as is done in the floodlit night scenes of the FSA documentarians.

Music, or at least the choice of it, added another element that diminished the film's realistic thrust despite the fact that the score by Fox musical director Alfred Newman avoids the soaring strings of the studio orchestra common to most Hollywood productions and incorporates traditional folk songs, notably an accordian rendition of "Red River Valley." This may initially seem a realistic use of folk material, but "Red River Valley" represents nostalgia for both the charac-ters and the audience. The unstated lyrics hang over many key scenes; "Please remember the Red River Valley," or in Fordian terms, hearken back nostalgically to what can be no more, the little farm in Oklahoma.

Two other technical areas of the film adaptation are definite minuses. In general, the sound is not of good quality, even considering the sound problems of that era. It is often fuzzy when it should be crisp, and soft where it should be loud and clear. More importantly, the visual editing of the final print is very rough. Robert Simpson, the chief editor, was another studio journeyman, equivalent to Nunnally Johnson in his professional attitude toward his work. However, the editing seems to have been rushed to get the picture out. In addition, Ford did not oversee the editing as he usually did; instead he went off on vacation, leaving Simpson and Zanuck to hack up his print in their hurry to finish the project. As a result there are problems of continuity, especially in the middle of the film, and even major discrepancies.

On the plus side of the artistic ledger is the almost perfect acting. Given the large number of characters, almost all the cast are supporting players, but the major dramatic tension exists in the relationship between Tom Joad (Henry Fonda) and Ma Joad (Jane Darwell). Ford had just directed Fonda in *Young Mr. Lincoln* (1939) and *Drums Along The Mohawk* (1939), and he sensed in the young actor the kind of quiet, American strength the part called for, a strength repeated over the years in many other films including Ford's *My Darling Clementine* (1946). (Fonda, who became a close friend of Steinbeck's, considered the role of Tom Joad his favorite performance.) Jane Darwell, a supporting actress for most of her career, turned in her best performance as the matriarch of the Joad clan. Although she proves a bit less fierce than Steinbeck's Ma, her sad eyes summed up the trials of the decade. She won the Academy Award for Best Supporting Actress, the only one of the cast to take an Oscar. (Henry Fonda undoubtedly deserved one, but it went to James Stewart for his performance in *The Philadelphia Story*, George Cukor's film adaptation of Philip Barry's comedy of manners.)

Like Jane Darwell, the rest of the cast were veteran supporting players, many part of Ford's "repertory" group, who were obviously inspired by their material. John Carradine simply *is* Jim Casy; after seeing the film it is impossible to imagine any other. Russell Simpson as Pa Joad, Frank Darien as Uncle John, and John Qualen as Muley Graves are also perfect evocations of the characters they represent, though Charley Grapewin as Grampa tends to overdo it a bit. Only the children, including Shirley Mills and Darryl Hickman as the Joad kids, Ruthie and Winfield, don't quite fit; they simply are too sleek and glowing to be the offspring of starving migrant workers.

Filming took place in October and November 1940 with most of the action shot on the 20th Century-Fox backlot. A second unit did location work along the migrant routes, shooting under the cover title, *Route 66*, to avoid confrontations with local authorities. Swiftly edited, the movie opened on January 24, 1940 to rave reviews and turn away crowds. Easily recouping its $750,000 cost, it eventually became one of the studio's top grossers of the period. Ford won the Oscar for Best Direction, though the movie lost out for Best Picture to Alfred Hitchock's melodramatic *Rebecca*.

An acknowledged classic, *The Grapes of Wrath* merits its reputation despite its ultimate failure to translate the full meaning of Steinbeck's novel to the screen. Though this relative failure can in some measure be attributed to the problems of institutions and personalities indicated above—certainly, Hollywood was not ready in 1940 to communicate Steinbeck's harsh message—part of the problem resides in the differences between the two mediums. For example, Steinbeck's opening chapter on Dust Bowl conditions, the first of the interchapters, would be hard to film except as a mini-documentary similar to Pare Lorentz's *The Plow That Broke the Plains* (1936). Lorentz's classic makes a fine half hour presentation, but on this scale, a full-blown version of Steinbeck's novel would require some fifteen hours of viewing. Even *War and Peace* could not support this scale, as the 1968 Soviet production demonstrated.

But scale is not the only problem, and Ford had to confront the essential difference between literary and filmic imagery. For example, Steinbeck's first sentence reads: "To the red country and part of the gray country of Oklahoma, the last rains came gently, and they did not cut the scarred earth"

(3).[13] The adjective "scarred" refers to the erosion patterns in the once fertile fields; these can and often were seen in 1930s documentaries, but the implied metaphor, the personification of "Mother Earth" actually cut and scarred, resides in the word itself. Though voice-over narration could have been used, there was always the danger that dependence on this technique would have ended in Steinbeck's long novel being read to the movie audience.

Obviously, the film adapter, like the literary translator, faces innumerable choices which affect the final meaning of the work. A close reading of the filmic text reveals some of the choices made in John Ford's *The Grapes of Wrath*.

After the credits, backed by the strains of "Red River Valley," Ford opens the film with a beautiful long shot of a man trudging over the horizon and down a lonely country road. The road is presented as a vertical plane which bisects the equally flat plane of the horizon; bisecting telephone lines repeat these angles. The man will soon be identified as Tom Joad, but as film critic Janey Place has noted, at this point he is "a nameless, faceless everyman."[14] He is one with the anonymous Dust Bowl refugees of Steinbeck's first chapter, for the scene suggests the desolation on the land. Not all the complexity of Steinbeck's first chapter can be captured in a few frames, but certainly Ford's quick transition to Chapter Two, the beginning of the Joad story, creates a great deal of the same feeling. Place argues that Ford's use of this vertical road motif engenders a sense of movement, of travel down the road of life toward the future.

As he trudges toward the highway crossroad and a truck stop cafe, Tom Joad is approaching a symbolic crossroads in his life. He has just been paroled from the state prison, where he has served four years for killing a man in self-defense during a drunken brawl at a country dance. Will he be able to set his life moving on the right track again? Ford presents most of Chapter Two, which concerns Tom's ride in a truck down the highway toward the Joad home place.

The ride prefigures the longer journey of the novel, and it subtly indicates the judgmental attitudes of society in the conversation between Tom and the truck driver. The driver is a "get ahead" type, tied to the world of the machine and displaced from natural relationships. The truck itself is the first of a number of menacing machines which Steinbeck employs as symbols of a threatening technology. Not that Steinbeck is an anti-technologist. The Joads are constantly connected with a machine, their cut down Hudson Super Six, but they humanize the machine by integrating it into their lives. When Al Joad is driving: "He had become the soul of the car"(167). And when Tom changes a piston on the side of the road, the process becomes almost an act of creativity. It is the unnatural, inhuman use of technology which Steinbeck indicts.

Chapter Three of the novel, the next interchapter, is omitted entirely from the film. This is thematically unfortunate because the indomitable land turtle described crawling across the highway suggests the movement of the Joads; the turtle carries a wild oat seed across the expanse of concrete just as they carry new life to California along Route 66. One driver, a woman, swerves to avoid the turtle; another, a truck driver, swerves to strike it. The truck spins the turtle across the road like a "tiddleywink," but the tough old fellow continues on his way, much as the Joads carry on in the face of adversity.

The next chapter of the novel—Tom's return home—is recreated almost entire in the film. This seems a bit puzzling as Tom's meeting with expreacher Jim Casy and their ensuing conversations are rather drawn out even in the novel. As his initials suggest, Casy is a Christ figure. A former holiness preacher, he has found a more abstract religion, a combination of the American traditions of Transcendentalism and Pragmatism, which in turn evolves into a sort of idealistic Socialism. Casy's major function is as mentor for Tom, to turn him from a reckless young ex-con into a responsible leader of the people. In both the novel and the film Tom and

Casy discuss their experiences and beliefs, as well the plight of the Joad family and the land they have toiled.

This plight becomes clear when Ford shows them walking to the Joad's abandoned farm, again beautifully photographed against the sky. In the novel this action opens Chapter Six. Chapter Five is a rather long interchapter that spells out in very specific terms how the rape of the land has led to dispossession of the people. Like *The Plow That Broke the Plains*, Steinbeck's novel uses images of machinery, "snubnosed monsters," making war on the land. "Behind the harrows, the long seeders—twelve curved iron penes erected in the foundry, orgasms set by gears, raping methodically, raping without passion."(49) The man who manages the machinery becomes "a part of the monster, a robot"(48). Ford dramatizes some of this material by transposing it to the reminiscences of Muley Graves, a neighbor of the Joads' who has lingered on after his family has left for California. Tom and Casy meet Muley in the darkened farm house, lit only by a match and then a candle. Though striking, this available light photography tends to be distracting in its artfulness. The same could be said of Ford's tractor scenes, which use a variety of camera tricks such as superimposition.

The scene of Muley's dispossession proves powerful, however, in its use of extreme angles to isolate the driver of the monstrous tractor and the dirt farmer close to his native earth. In one of the film's most powerful shots, the camera looks down on Muley squatting to feel the soil, saying: "Being born on it, and workin' on it, an' dying on it—thats what makes it ourn, not a piece of paper."[15] The flashback ends with an image of Muley's family as shadows, as the camera looks over them at the retiring tractor.

Muley reveals that much the same fate has been visited on the Joads, who have moved on to the home of their Uncle John. Tom and Casy decide to spend the night in the deserted house, but the arrival of the land company's deputies sends them scurrying across the darkened fields in another scene heightened by interesting light patterns. The crisscrossing

headlights and spotlights of the cars searching for them in the
fields suggest the evitable conflict between the people of the
land and its institutional exploiters.

The walk to Uncle John's, again with Tom and Casy
outlined against the sky, introduces the next major sequence,
the immediate preparations for the California trip. Omitting
Steinbeck's short chapter describing the used car lots in the
hyped-up language of used car salesmen, Ford proceeds to the
reunion of Tom and his family. In both the novel and the film
this long sequence serves essentially to introduce the others
who are to participate in this saga. Ford changes the order of
introduction, appropriately putting Ma, who has become the
matriarch of the family, first. The men have been shocked by
their dislocation from the farms that had given them their
identities. The women have been forced to become stronger,
and Ma as conceived by John Steinbeck and portrayed by
Jane Darwell is one of the strongest. We also meet Pa Joad
and Uncle John; Grampa and Granma; Ruthie and Winfield,
the youngest Joad children; Noah, Tom's strange older
brother; Al, his feisty teenage brother, and Tom's sister
Rosasharn and her new husband, Connie Rivers. The preparations for leaving involve some of the materials from the
interchapters, especially Chapter Nine, in which the selection
of the belongings to take along and those to leave behind is
made. One of the latter is in the family's second favorite book
Pilgrim's Progress. (The first is the Bible.) Ford creates a
beautiful scene as Ma sorts through her own mementoes,
stopping to hold her best earrings up to the mirror. In the
background the muted strains of "Red River Valley" un-
derscore the poignancy of the scene.

The morning scene offers a change of pace. Grampa,
completely alienated by the move from his own land, refuses
to leave. Afraid to take him by force, the Joads get him drunk
on alcoholic cough medicine in one of the film's few comic
scenes. Though the novel contains a great deal of humor,
especially verbal humor, in the film most of this material was

evidently scrapped in order to avoid censorship problems and to keep the central story moving.

And move it does, as a montage of road signs and scenes condenses much of the material from the novel's road chapters, the second major part of the plot. Steinbeck contrasts two documentary chapters, Chapter Eleven on the abandoned farm houses and Chapter Twelve on the road, Route 66. Both have the feel of the FSA documentary photographs featuring the empty shacks left behind and the crowded wrecks creeping on toward California. Ford is very selective here, choosing to dramatize only a few events to get the feel of the road. An important moment for the family is Grampa's death of a stroke before they even leave Oklahoma—as Casy remarks, he finally couldn't leave his own land. Because they have no money to spare for a funeral, the family buries Grampa in a roadside field, his grave marked only with a note in an old fruit jar. Ford translates this moving scene effectively, with Toland's chiaroscuro lighting effects adding much to the meaning of this tragic moment in the lives of the Joads.

The family has begun to disintegrate under the pressure of change. In the novel, Steinbeck balances the loss of the family elder with the addition of the Wilsons, an older couple who helped to bury the Grandpa. They agree to share their old Dodge with the Joads in return for help with its mechanical problems. Thus as the nuclear family collapses, the larger, more universal family of humankind becomes more important. The Wilsons are eliminated from the movie, justifiably in terms of plot complication, but at some loss of thematic clarity. This loss is increased by the excision of Chapter Fourteen, an interchapter describing the new cooperation between the migrants in striking biological imagery. This long passage is worth quoting as it demonstrates Steinbeck's sense of the total ecology of his scene.

> One man, one family driven from the land; this rusty car creaking along the highway to the west. I lost my land; a

single tractor took my land. I am alone and I am bewil-
dered. And in the night one family camps in a ditch and
another family pulls in and the tents come out. The two men
squat on their hams and the women and the children listen.
Here is the node, you who hate change and fear revolution.
Keep these two squatting men apart; make them hate, fear,
suspect each other. Here is the anlage of the thing you fear.
This is the zygote. For here "I lost my land" is changed; a
cell is split and from its splitting grows the thing you
hate—"We lost *our* land."(206)

Humankind replicates nature in its evolution, from a single
family to a larger social organization. Though he fails to make
use of this interchapter, Ford dramatizes a sentimental parable (Chapter Fifteen) illustrating something of the same point
of human community. Even the change from a documentary
interchapter to the Joad narrative shows Ford's diminution of
the universal themes.

Before this more positive scene Ford does stress the
Joads' difficult situation by presenting a warning from a
backtracking Okie who has been defeated by conditions in
California. This order reverses that of the novel, but seems
necessary because of the excision of the harsh warnings
implied in Chapter Fourteen. In the film, the warning is
another beautifully composed night scene, full of menacing
shadows from which the tragic Okie, who has lost his family
to starvation, emerges and eventually disappears. The Joads
are shaken, but they remain committed to the California trip.
There can be no turning back now.

Their faith is somewhat strengthened when at a roadside
hamburger stand, they are received with sympathy and
charity. Mae, the prototype of sassy café waitresses, not only
gives the Joads an extra measure of bread for their money,
but provides candy for the children at a discount. The Joads
are unaware of this, but Mae's rough and ready truck driver
customers have taken it all in and reward her with a substantial tip. This cinematic dramatization of the biblical injunc-

tion to cast one's bread upon the waters, follows the novel closely, but omits an unfeeling wealthy couple—referred to as "shitheels" by Mae—and a good deal of the characters' verbal cynicism, including the remarks of the tough fry cook who compares the waitress' tip bonanza to a slot machine payoff. Ford's retention of this rather sentimental scene in preference to many harsher ones, is indicative of his overall thematic emphasis.

Another roadway montage condenses the action of Chapters Sixteen and Seventeen. In addition to omitting the scene in which Tom repairs the Wilsons' ancient Dodge, Ford excises the even more significant moment in which Ma defies Pa and Tom in order to keep the family together—a fierce assertion of will would have nicely balanced the sentimentalizing of Jane Darwell's film role. Chapter Sixteen also contains the warning scene, which Ford presented before the hamburger stand parable. Evidently some footage was dropped in this badly edited section; for example, when they stop at the Colorado River crossing into California, Noah simply disappears.

Ford picks up the action of the novel with a night drive across the desert which culminates in Grandma's death. In both novel and film Ma conceals the old woman's death so that the family can get past the border guards into the promised land of California. Ford handles the revelation beautifully. The family stop to view the green valley at dawn and all rush to the side of the road leaving Ma isolated in the car. Tom separates himself from the family to return to her and ultimately share her sorrowful burden.

Steinbeck's harsh analysis of California history is the subject of Chapter Nineteen. These remarks find some expression in Ford's film when the Joads meet an Oklahoma-born California policeman (played by Ford regular Ward Bond) who exchanges friendly reminiscences but warns them to be out of town by nightfall. The film then follows Chapter Twenty of the novel, the family's introduction to "Hooverville," the first of the roadside migrant camps which will become their homes. Here Toland's camera follows a long tracking shot duplicating the Joads' viewpoint as they slowly drive through the camp. The influence of the documentary photographers is most evident in the composition of this scene of roadside squalor as the Joads and the audience are graphically introduced to the harsh reality of their situation.

This note is maintained in the scene in which Ma tries to feed her family. Dozens of the camp children surround them, not asking directly, but obviously hoping to be fed. Ma tries to perform a miracle by sharing her meager rations with the group. Here there is no immediate return, for the dinner scene is followed by a fight and a shooting which leaves an Okie woman badly wounded by a trigger-happy deputy. Casy surprisingly rises to the occasion and knocks the deputy out. He stays to be sent off to jail, taking on himself the blame that might fall on the camp.

In both novel and film this action proves the turning point for Casy: he changes completely from the minister of the Lord to the minister of the People. Another member leaves the Joads to swell the universal family; Casy will become one of its leaders. That night the family moves on as the deputies—self-appointed vigilantes in the film—come back to clean out "Hooverville." In the novel, the Joads move to a more orderly government camp at Weedpatch, then leave for the company camp at a peach orchard, and finally take shelter from winter floods in the abandoned box cars at a cotton camp.

The film reverses this order by having them first journey to the peach orchard camp, then to the government camp, then out once more onto the open road. This transposition entirely changes the novel's thematic statement. Instead of promising hope, descending to bleakness, and rising to hope again, the film optimistically moves forward from the moment of the disappointing arrival in California. The effect of this reordering of the narrative scenes is increased by the omission of the later documentary chapters, all of which graphically point up the prevailing economic injustices: Chapter Twenty-One, an indictment of factory farms; Chapter Twenty-Three, an account of the people's simple pleasures; Chapter Twenty-Five, a frightening picture of food destroyed to maintain produce prices[16]; Chapter Twenty-Seven, a condemnation of the cotton farms, and Chapter Twenty-Nine, a bleak vision of the miseries brought by winter. All five chapters are virtually ignored in the film. Chapter Twenty-Five contains the source of the novel's title: "In the souls of the people the grapes of wrath are filling and growing heavy, growing heavy for the vintage"(477).

Even the narrative chapters are pruned of their more controversial aspects. For example, when in the novel a migrant is asked for a definition of a Red, he repeats one he heard from a landowner: "A Red is any son-of-a-bitch that wants thirty cents an hour when we're paying twenty-five"(407). In the film his reply is: "Brother, I don't know." All of these changes, large and small, combine to considerably distort Steinbeck's intentions.

Following the order of the film, the next sequence translates Chapter Twenty-Six of the novel, the action at the peach ranch. This is an important development for in the course of the action Tom will be reunited with Casy and eventually becomes his successor in leadership. The arrival at the peach camp repeats the hard, documentary look of the "Hooverville" camp. The Joads and the others are unwitting strikebreakers, admitted to the camp only to keep wages down. The family soon discovers the inadequacy of the wage scale when after a half-day's work, they have not earned enough to buy dinner. Tom decides to investigate the situation and sneaks out of the armed camp to talk with the strikers. He finds they are led by Casy, who urges him to join them. Before Tom can decide, another vigilante attack sends the strike leaders scurrying. Tom and Casy hide under a bridge, but they are discovered. Casy dies insisting that "You guys don't know

what you're doing." After the Christ figure's martyrdom, Tom
accepts his role as leader and kills a vigilante. Although badly
hurt, he manages to crawl back to the family's cabin. The
whole fight sequence is the dramatic, as well as the thematic
climax of the film, and it is brilliantly presented in patterns of
bright lights and black shadows.

In another night scene, the Joads manage to smuggle
Tom out of the camp, and they make their way to the
government camp, Weedpatch, conveniently renamed
"Wheatpatch" in the movie. The camp is run by a genial FDR
look-alike (Grant Mitchell) who welcomes the Joads like long
lost kinfolk. In general, the film seems to present the camp as
a liberal answer to the migrant's problems. Steinbeck, who
had stayed at one of these government camps certainly
approved of them, but the film seems to posit indoor plumb-
ing as a social goal, while the novel forces a reconsideration of
the entire economic system. The government camp interlude
forms Chapters Twenty-Two and Twenty-Four of the novel,
which are largely reproduced in the film.

In fact Ford even elaborates on the action, making much
of the country dance only sketched in the novel. Steinbeck
includes the dance as a symbol of the people's solidarity
against vigilante attempts to break it up, but for Ford dances
are symbols of an almost mystical harmony, and in the film
his vision supersedes Steinbeck's. The dancing, mostly to the
tune of "Red River Valley," is extended considerably, and
after a turn with Ma, Tom takes his tearful leave by the side of
the empty dance platform. Tom's parting speech stays close
to that in the novel, and the film emphasizes his transfigura-
tion by having him walk across the empty dance floor and off
into the distance. In a replication of the film's opening, he is
last seen in a very long shot, a tiny figure climbing a hill,
outlined against the brightening dawn.[17]

The film's major narrative change from the novel is the
complete abandonment of Steinbeck's conclusion. Not only
are Steinbeck's documentary chapters of the California sec-

tion dropped, but so are the events of the narrative—Chapters Twenty-eight and Thirty, in which the Joads are reduced to utter misery. In the novel, after they sneak off from the peach strike, Tom leaves, again weakening the nuclear family structure. The remaining Joads proceed to a cotton farm, where they encounter the worst conditions yet. Their plight deteriorates further as winter sets in, bringing cold, rain, and floods. At the end of the novel, wet, cold, and nearly starving, the Joads seek shelter in a farmer's barn. Here they encounter the equally wretched Wainwrights, and Rosasharn gives her milk swollen breasts to the dying old man. The novel ends on this biological affirmation of the life force and human affirmation of the force of charity in creating a larger conception of "family."

Ford's film ends with the Joads leaving the government camp with the promise of twenty days work to the north. As they drive off, the scene recalls their departure from Oklahoma. They have discovered no promised land; their dreams are shattered; the family is disintegrating. Yet Ma is still capable of a speech of affirmation.

> "I know," Ma chuckled. "Maybe that makes us tough. Rich fellas come up an' they die, an' their kids ain't no good, an' they die out. But, Tom, we keep a-coming! Don't you fret none, Tom. A different time's comin'."

The speech comes from Chapter Twenty of the novel, when the Joads left their first camp in "Hooverville."

Of course, at that point they still had hope for the future, hope that was partially justified by the relatively pleasant stay at the government camp. To transpose the speech to the end of the California section, to the conclusion of the story, wrenches it out of context and changes the thrust of both Ma's speech and Steinbeck's ending.

The imagery of Ford's conclusion is still viable, however. Ma's speech is genuinely moving as Jane Darwell delivers it, backed by the strains of "Red River Valley." The last shot is another vertical road stretching out into the American future, a scene which can stand for the whole film in a sense. John Ford's *The Grapes of Wrath* is a beautiful, moving, and intelligent film, though not the great novel which John Steinbeck wrote.

IV. THE FORGOTTEN VILLAGE

The documentary thrust of Steinbeck's prewar work was confirmed by the two creative projects which followed *The Grapes of Wrath*. In 1941 he coauthored with Ed Ricketts a nonfiction book, *Sea of Cortez: A Leisurely Journal of Travel and Research*, and he wrote the screenplay for Herbert Kline's documentary film, *The Forgotten Village*. Both works are concerned with Mexico. "Sea of Cortez" was Steinbeck's poetic name for the Gulf of California, and the book so titled is the record of a six-week voyage the author made in the Gulf with Ricketts. Ostensibly, they went to study the invertebrate marine life of the Gulf, but much of their time was spent relaxing, sightseeing, and talking. Steinbeck wrote an informal "log" of the trip, which included philosophical views sharpened during long friendly talks; Ricketts provided the scientific apparatus for the book. (In 1951, Steinbeck's "log" was republished without the scientific data; but with a memoir of Ed Ricketts.) *Sea of Cortez* remains an interesting, readable book, and one which reveals much about Steinbeck's ideas at the apex of his career.

"The design of a book is the pattern of a reality controlled and shaped by the mind of the writer. This is completely understood about poetry or fiction, but it is seldom understood about books of fact. And yet the impulse which drives a man to poetry will send another man into the tide pools and force him to report on what he finds there" (69).[1] Emphasizing the balance between the documentary and creative impulses of nonfiction, the author goes on to say:

"We wanted to see everything our eyes would accommodate, to think what we could, and, out of seeing and thinking, to build some kind of structure in modeled imitation of the observed reality" (70).

This neat statement of the documentary principle could serve as introduction to *The Grapes of Wrath* or *The Forgotten Village* as well as to *Sea of Cortez*. Later in the book Steinbeck evolves his most careful statement of his nonteleological theory. Simply put, nonteleology demands that things be seen as they are, rather than as they "could or should or might be" (139). Obviously this philosophy implies a documentary method, and later Steinbeck calls nonteology a *"modus operandi . . .* a method of handling data of any sort"* (150). The importance of *Sea of Cortez* in understanding Steinbeck's sense of documentary mode, form, and style is generally overlooked by most critics who stress only the book's subject matter.

The Forgotten Village can be viewed as a concrete example of the theories presented in the *Sea of Cortez*. Steinbeck became involved in the project when friends introduced him to Herbert Kline, a distinguished young director of documentary films.[2] Kline had just directed four anti-fascist films: *Heart of Spain* (1937), *Return to Life* (1938), *Crisis* (1939), *Lights Out In Europe* (1940). He now asked Steinbeck to write a screenplay about a threatened military coup in Mexico.[3] By the time Kline arrived in Mexico to plan the film, the coup had been crushed; however, he came across another story: the conflict between the ancient *curanderas*, or folk healers, and the modern practitioners of medicine. After five weeks of absorbing Mexican local color, Steinbeck then wrote a second screenplay in two weeks. Kline completed the film in Mexico after Steinbeck left, though the author returned for at least part of the shooting and the post-production work. His agents also arranged for Viking's publication (1941) of a documentary book drawn from the film. After a succession of problems with the music, the narration, and censorship, the film finally

opened on November 18, 1941, to good reviews and a modest
public response.[4] Unfortunately, Pearl Harbor quickly de-
flected interest from the work, which was, however, to win
two postwar awards.[5]

The Forgotten Village deserved a better fate. Although its
social message has aged poorly, it is an interesting example of
a phase in the development of both the documentary film and
Steinbeck's career. The writer, continuing in the mode of his
recent fiction, created a unique combination of documentary
and parable, a balance which he was rarely to achieve in his
later work. In his "Preface" to the documentary book, Steinbeck indicates that his method will parallel that of The Grapes
of Wrath. Instead of depicting a great mass of people, the film
will concentrate on one symbolic family, a sort of case history
that will demonstrate a universal truth. He wrote what he
calls an "elastic" story and then stretched it to fit the
circumstances the film team found when they moved into a
real back country village. The people of the pueblo were the
cast, the place itself the set. A narrator told the story, as none
of the villagers could speak Spanish, much less English.
Finally Steinbeck says: "We did not editorialize, attack, or
defend anything. We put on film what we found, only arrang-
ing it to make a coherent story."[6] Obviously the nonteleological method announced in Sea of Cortez was intended to form
The Forgotten Village.

Unfortunately, Steinbeck and his filmic coauthors did
not follow their own program. The Forgotten Village, for all its
strengths, is essentially an editorial, an attack on folk cures
and a defense of modern medicine. In Mexico of 1940 such an
editorial was socially desirable; from the perspective of 1980s
this stance seems debatable, if not simplistic. Contemporary
views neither accept scientific medicine so unquestioningly,
nor scorn folk medicine so completely. Interestingly enough,
in 1940 the only critic to take this view was Steinbeck's friend
and mentor, the thoughtful scientist Ed Ricketts. In an
unpublished piece which he called an "anti-script" to The

Forgotten Village, Ricketts questions the assumption of scientific and technological progress underlying the film. Ricketts asserted that, ". . . in an inward sense the Mexicans are more advanced than we are."[7] Recent developments in ecology, holistic medicine, and natural cures, tend to support Ricket's suspicion of Steinbeck's scienticism in the film. An interesting comparison can be made with Chicano novelist Rudolph Anaya's *Bless Me, Ultima* (1974), the story of how a Chicano boy discovers his real roots through instruction from his Mexican grandmother, who is a *curandera.* Ricketts anti-script proposed a similar story with a young boy instructed by a wise old man.

This problem of theme weakens *The Forgotten Village* in toto; the story becomes too pat, the parable too obvious. The opening establishes the setting, the mountain pueblo of Santiago, as well as the cast of characters, the central symbolic family. The family consists of parents, Ventura and Esperanza, seven unmarried daughters and three sons: little Paco, teenaged Carlos, and Juan Diego, who is nearing manhood. Juan Diego becomes the protagonist as he bridges the generation gap in the village created by the sudden arrival of modern technology. In the first scene Juan Diego has brought his mother, who is heavy with another child, to see Trini, the *curandera.* Both mother and son accept the "Wise Woman's" prediction of a healthy male child, and Juan Diego brings the good news to his father, who is shown harvesting the corn crop. Later when the crops are brought in to be sold, the eldest son's emerging independence is demonstrated when he questions the owner's division of the harvest. Clearly this young man does not blindly accept traditional authority. He has been to the new government school, named for Francisco Madero, the first revolutionary President of Mexico. The school, the idealistic young teachers, and finally the student, Juan Diego, are all committed to advancing the goals of the Revolution through modernization.

After the harvest is sold, the family sets off for market

day in a nearby town. These scenes of public ceremonies are among the strongest in the film. In general, director Kline maintains a documentary stance toward his materials. For the most part, his subjects are captured from eye level and at medium distance. Occasional long shots establish the relationships between the characters and their natural environment, much as in *The Grapes of Wrath,* and occasional close-ups underline symbolic details. Yet the film essentially is a studied documentary in style. Kline was evidently determined to guard against the influence of Sergei Eisenstein's *Que Viva Mexico!* with its Expressionist renderings of the same settings.[8] Some Eisensteinian touches are evident, but a more important stylistic factor is the subject matter itself. Although presented in realistic fashion, the inherent romanticism of the exotic environment creates a kind of counterpoint to Kline's efforts. The miniature bullfight, fought by a tiny matador against his dog decorated with artificial horns, is a good example of this conflict.

The vitality of the young matador contrasts with the strange, listless behavior of little Paco, who has a stomach ache. When the family returns home after the market day, Paco worsens, and they send for the *curandera.* She attempts a cure with ancient magic, using a symbolic egg to draw the pain from the child's stomach. Skeptical Juan Diego has heard of other children sickening in the same way, and he goes to confer with his schoolteacher after Trini fails to achieve results.

The teacher suspects that the water supply is contaminated, but the superstitious villagers reject this notion and maintain their faith in ancient healers. Trini is called to Paco's aid once more; again her cure fails, and this time the boy dies. The atmosphere of the child's wake and funeral are powerfully evoked by the play of light and shadow over saddened, pain-worn faces and grotesque religious icons. The funeral is then contrasted with a birth scene almost as striking. The shock of Paco's death has brought his mother to early labor, in which she is attended by Trini as midwife. This was the scene censored by the New York Board of Review but later restored on appeal. It seems far from shocking today, especially as the birth was clearly feigned.

The fiesta of Santiago, or St. James, the village patron saint, provides an interlude between tragedies. Especially interesting in these scenes is the mock combat between "Castilians and Moors" acted out by the costumed villagers. The religious procession, with a life-size crucifix, attempts to win the intercession of the saint for the sick children of the village. Juan Diego and the teacher take a more practical course. They show the villagers a film on disease and propose a petition to seek medical aid. The village elders reject the proposal, and when Juan Diego challenges them, the village chief strikes him. When one of his little sisters sickens, Juan sets out on foot for Mexico City to obtain medical help.

The camera follows him through the streets of the capital to the hospital where he is able to convince a medical team to return with him. However, the *curandera* turns the people against them, and the villagers hide their children. After the medical team has purified the well, Trini convinces the crowd that they have actually poisoned the water. The village rises up against the visitors and drives them out with curses and blows. The ancient *curandera* strikes Juan Diego, accusing him of bringing misfortune to the people. Undaunted, Juan Diego defies both his father and tradition. Stealing back to the village, he gives his sister a healing injection. The teacher comforts him when his father turns him out of the house; Juan Diego will return to Mexico City with the medical team and begin the study of medicine. The final scenes are shot in the laboratories of the University Medical School and they conclude with a close-up of Juan Diego, dedicated to the mission of bringing modern medicine to his people.

The film's conclusion recalls many 1930s documentary and feature films that promised much from the miracles of science and technology. Certainly, Steinbeck and Kline were right to stress the importance of adequate medical care for poor peasants, yet their out-of-hand dismissal of folk medicine and religious traditions now seems less acceptable. All in all, this short film fails to strike a balance between progress and tradition. As a result the story now seems simplistic and the characters one-dimensional. Four decades later what strikes us as best in the film is its documentary report on a complex culture in a moment of change and crisis. As such it is important for its demonstrations of Steinbeck's interest in both documentary form and in Mexico, a setting he would return to in *The Pearl* and *Viva Zapata!*, his best postwar works.

V. THE END OF AN ERA

Although *The Grapes of Wrath* was released as a film in 1940 and *The Forgotten Village* in 1941, they definitely belong in the discussion of the Depression Decade. The novel and film versions of *The Grapes of Wrath* were the culmination of Steinbeck's development in the 1930s, not just in terms of popular but of artistic success. The *Sea of Cortez* and *The Forgotten Village* were smaller works which can serve as glosses on his major achievements.

Steinbeck's philosophy of nonteleology and his own documentary film demonstrate the importance the decade's realistic thrust to his artistic vision. The author's published works from 1929 to 1935 look backward toward nineteenth-century Romanticism and early Modernism; the influence of 1920s best sellers is obvious in these apprentice fictions. Even his first popular success, *Tortilla Flat* in 1935, proves basically sentimental, its literary interest deriving principally from the romantic matter of Arthurian legend imposed on the *paisanos* of Monterey. *In Dubious Battle*, which appeared a year later, provided the prototype for the popular and literary achievements of the late 1930s. *Of Mice and Men* (1937), *The Long*

Valley (1938), and *The Grapes of Wrath* (1939) made Steinbeck the representative writer of his decade.

Because he combined a sensitive talent for the tale, the epic, and the romance with an objective, impersonal, and realistic vision of America in the 1930s, Steinbeck created the most persuasive of images of the American Dream gone sour. Derived from the overall documentary thrust of the decade, his artistic vision was itself to become a major influence. Not yet forty years old in 1941, John Steinbeck was already considered the most important writer in America.

3

The War Years

I. A NEW DECADE

Less than a month after *The Forgotten Village* finally reached the screen and *Sea of Cortez* was published, the Japanese bombed Pearl Harbor and America was at war. The onset of World War II profoundly altered John Steinbeck's career. During the war years he seemed to be in a holding pattern, trying to adjust to his earlier success and to understand the cataclysmic events around him. He wanted to develop as an artist, to attempt new subjects and forms, but on every side this development was inhibited by the events, both public and personal, of the new decade. He made several new starts, but he was never again to regain his artistic momentum.

Steinbeck's career stalled for many reasons. The mood of American culture changed with the advent of war, as the Depression decade's objective reassessment of the American Dream was transformed under wartime pressures into a reaffirmation of American traditions and ideals. Objective observation and realistic analysis were replaced by sentimental idealism and patriotic propaganda as truth inevitably became "the first casualty." Even the documentary films of the period were propagandistic rather than analytic. Literature followed this new model, when it did not completely give way to Hollywood sentimentality.

Steinbeck's work—his fiction, drama, and film writing—proved no exception to these general tendencies. The literary quality, if not the popularity, of his work inexorably declined, and he seemed unable to reverse this trend. He had switched from one film model, the artistic documentary, to its antithesis, the Hollywood melodrama. However, not only the style but the subject matter of his work proved a problem.

Steinbeck's best writing had evolved out of his own observation and experience. He had established himself as a serious writer when he discovered the material of the Salinas Valley, and his great works of the late 1930s came out of personal involvement with their subjects. In the 1940s Steinbeck quite naturally wanted to write about the war, though he had no direct experience of it. Written out of imagined experiences, his fictional works of the period now seem inauthentic, while his attempt at direct involvement as a war correspondent produced only journalistically competent dispatches. Eventually, he turned back to his weakest material from the 1930s, the sentimental observation of colorful outcasts in Monterey. All in all, he was unable to come to terms with the war, the central experience of the new decade, in either an artistic or a personal sense.

Personal considerations began to affect Steinbeck's work. He had turned forty early in 1942, and the decade saw important changes in his life. Most significantly, Steinbeck divorced his first wife, Carol Henning, and married Gwen Conger in 1943.[1] The divorce was bitter and the monetary settlement punitive.[2]

His second wife was a beautiful aspiring actress, a good deal younger than himself. She met Steinbeck following the success of *The Grapes of Wrath,* and she evidently expected to share the life style of a successful and affluent author. No doubt she directly influenced his decision to move from California to New York. (They had two sons, Steinbeck's only children, and when they finally divorced in 1948, he had to make another disadvantageous financial settlement.) Steinbeck's life style more and more resembled that of a movie star, not a writer.

Following the success of *Tortilla Flat* in 1935 Steinbeck
had received offers to write for Hollywood. Although friends
like novelist John O'Hara urged him to take advantage of the
easy money, he had continued to resist the blandishments of
the movie colony.[3] Almost instinctively, he seemed to fear
success as much as failure, as though sensing that money and
applause would tend to corrupt his personal vision. *The
Forgotten Village* was his first work written directly for the
screen, and he did it for a share of the film's meager profits
rather than take the $5,000 a week Darryl F. Zanuck report-
edly offered him to write for Twentieth Century-Fox.[4] Suddenly, he was in urgent need of the large sums that only
Hollywood could pay. On a more subtle level, he perhaps also
needed the sense of being even more squarely in the limelight.
A popular writer, author of best sellers and smash stage and
screenplays, could be at the center of events; he could be the
friend of actors, sports stars, and politicians. Thus, Steinbeck's personal life confirmed a direction which his career
was already taking.

Steinbeck's works of 1942—fictional, dramatic, filmic,
and documentary—all indicate the diffusion of purpose
which characterize this period of his career. Early in the year
he published *The Moon Is Down*. His first novel since *The
Grapes of Wrath* in 1939, it dealt unconvincingly with the Nazi
occupation of a small European town. Intellectual critics
decried the novel's lack of realism, its unmotivated characters, and its hackneyed plot. Patriotic critics complained that
it was too soft on the Nazi invaders, that by making them too
human Steinbeck might be inducing complaisance in the
wartime audience. These negative judgments did not deter
the book buying public, and the new novel's initial sales were
even larger than those for *The Grapes of Wrath*.[5] Steinbeck's
own dramatic version of the novel opened on Broadway in
April 1942. Panned by most critics, it ran only nine weeks but
was soon sold to the movies for a then phenomenal $300,000.[6]
(All three versions of this work will be dealt with in more

detail after the discussion of *Tortilla Flat* which appeared as a film in 1942.)

Steinbeck's major writing project of 1942 was *Bombs Away!*, a contribution to the war effort in the form of a documentary book on the training of a bomber crew. The writer traveled the country for several months gathering data for his book in the company of photographer John Swope. Then both combined their efforts in a straightforward record that traces the progress of the crew from green recruits to a precision team taking off on the final page for their first combat mission. Published by Viking to laudatory reviews and excellent sales, *Bombs Away!* was sold to the movies for $250,000, but it was never made into a film.[7] All profits on the book, including the author's royalties, were donated to the Air Forces Aid Society. Read today, the book, though competent enough, is mainly important for the evidences it contains of Steinbeck's changed attitudes. The 1930s are almost glossed over, as Steinbeck tells the reader that the war has united the country after the divisions of the Depression. Now the American tradition shines through again. Steinbeck says: "The young men of now are the equals of any young men in our history. The scouts and fighters of our past have their counterparts in the present."[8] These young men, we are told, have traditions of hardiness inherited from frontiersman, of mechanical ability inherited from tinkerers and inventors, of teamwork inherited from football and baseball heroes. He then closely describes the training of six disparate young men, each from a different part of the country, who come together to form a new American team, a bomber team who would bring the war home to the enemy.[9]

II. TORTILLA FLAT

The Steinbeck film of 1942 was *Tortilla Flat*, adapted from his novel published in 1935 and sold to the movies the same year.

Although Steinbeck cannot be held accountable for the film, as he played no part in the production, it nevertheless reflects the general direction of the writer's career during the war years: a return to his weakest material and manner. The condescension and sentimentality which engulf the screen version of *Tortilla Flat* flowered in Hollywood but were rooted in Steinbeck's novel.

His first best seller and his first property bought by Hollywood, *Tortilla Flat* represented the popularizing element in Steinbeck's work. In a sense the early success of the book may have established him as a writer, providing the means to create the great works of the late 1930s. Then the success of *The Grapes of Wrath* and the film made from it put *Tortilla Flat* on the screen. Its commercial success led in turn to another weak movie, *A Medal For Benny* (1945), adapted from an unpublished Steinbeck story that also concerned the *paisanos* of Monterey. The movie *Tortilla Flat* perhaps was an ill omen for Steinbeck's later career; it was clearly a diversion from the harsh realities of the war (which America was losing in 1942), and as such it prefigures Steinbeck's last novel of the war years, *Cannery Row* (1945)—a reprise of *Tortilla Flat* and a clear sign of Steinbeck's declining talents.[1]

Tortilla Flat is a difficult novel to characterize because Steinbeck mixed so many diverse elements in it. At the time, he was friendly with a teacher of Spanish at Monterey High School who knew the local *paisanos* quite well. She not only provided Steinbeck with dozens of colorful tales, but guided him through the environs of Tortilla Flat itself.[2] Steinbeck decided that this material would provide a relief from his more serious writing, in both subject and style. He would portray this colorful environment in a series of interrelated short stories, structured by a number of parallels with the tales of Malory's *Morte d'Arthur*. In a long letter to his agent he states: "The form is that of the Malory version, the coming of Arthur and the mystic quality of owning a house, the forming of the round table, the adventure of the knights and finally, the mystic translation of Danny."[3] The book combines his observation of California life with a complex allegorical understructure much like his earlier works.

As in his earlier novels, Steinbeck was not quite able to achieve a balance between these elements in *Tortilla Flat*. First of all, his grasp of the realistic materials was incomplete. Although he spoke some Spanish, he really did not know the *paisanos*. As a result, they often seem more like types inherited from other writers than closely observed or deeply felt characters. His vision of them was also impeded by racial stereotyping, a problem in his literary treatment of all minority groups. Not that Steinbeck was in any way a conscious racist; he simply retained the ordinary stereotypes developed in his background. His *paisanos* are variations of both stock "happy-go-lucky Mexicans" and literary "noble savages." This latter term seems more appropriate because Steinbeck appears to have intended his *paisanos* as foils for the American middle class, whose values he scorned.

The impression of racial condescension is heightened by Steinbeck's use of the Arthurian structuring device; it led him to a mock heroic stance that tends to weaken his characters. The Arthurian parallel also appears to have forced Steinbeck into an unsatisfactory conclusion to the novel—Danny's unmotivated madness and death.[4]

Though Steinbeck did not quite have the control of either his realistic or allegorical materials, *Tortilla Flat* is far from a failure. Never descending to the sentimentality of his fellow Californian William Saroyan in the depiction of colorful personalities, he created real—if somewhat limited—characters, and his story is consistently interesting, if occasionally unbelievable. Maintaining a nuanced ironic distance from the people and events he describes, he achieved a work which can still be read as a clever entertainment.

Most likely it was never intended to be read as more. In a letter to his agent, Steinbeck expressed surprise at *Tortilla Flat*'s sudden success. "Curious that this second-rate book, written for relaxation, should cause this fuss. People are actually taking it seriously."[5] Of course, it is not at all clear how serious the popular response really was. The reviews are full of phrases like "childlike natures," "lovable thieves," and "children of nature"—all of which seem to indicate that the public took the work as escapist diversion from the problems of the Depression. In a preface written for the 1937 Modern Library Edition of the novel Steinbeck somewhat unjustifiably attacks "literary slummers" who see the *paisanos* as "quaint." Despite this ambivalence, he must have been impressed with the money the book earned; as his economic needs increased, the temptation to repeat the formula and crank out another best seller must have been great indeed.

Tortilla Flat as a novel remains a problematic work in the Steinbeck canon; its artistic success is debatable, and certainly its popular success created as many problems for the writer as those its publication solved. But if the novel presents a problem in critical judgment, its film adaptation does not; the movie *Tortilla Flat*, it is safe to say, was an unmitigated failure of art. Unfortunately, its popular success probably tempted Steinbeck to adapt and repeat its sentimental excesses in later works, both literary and filmic.

Critics generally agree that the film's artistic problems are as much rooted in Steinbeck's novel as in the Hollywood system. The movie's creators merely appropriated the most banal and sentimental elements of Steinbeck's work, discarding anything that smacked of wit, irony, or psychological complexity. All in all, *Tortilla Flat* ranks as one of Hollywood's worst "class" productions of a competent literary property.

The blame for this screen failure must finally rest with the director, Victor Fleming, a Hollywood professional with a long list of major film credits. Fleming was an old Hollywood hand, and he came to the movie capital just as it was establishing itself. After working as a cameraman for such directorial greats as D. W. Griffith, Fleming directed his first feature in 1919. A prolific if generally undistinguished decade of silent films followed before Fleming hit his creative stride with an adaptation of Owen Wister's classic Western novel *The Virginian* (1929), the first important Western in the sound era. Over the next decade he made his mark with films like *Captains Courageous* (1937), *The Wizard of Oz* (1939), and *Gone With the Wind* (1939). These lavishly produced Hollywood classics create in the moviegoer legitimate expectations that are not rewarded in *Tortilla Flat*.

A closer look at Fleming's film credits suggest why. His best known films are all splashy adaptations of popular novels that met with even greater success after their translation to the screen. Literary complexity was not Fleming's forte, as *Dr. Jekyll and Mr. Hyde* (1941) and *Joan of Arc* (1949) obviously demonstrate. A studio director, he was often indifferent to the essential nature of a project, and even his best work owes much to the efforts of producers (David O. Selznick for *Gone With the Wind*), stars (Judy Garland in *The Wizard of Oz*), or the technical staff (in both of the above). *Tortilla Flat* was unfortunately a film to which no one of talent was very seriously committed.

Perhaps the most interested party was Benjamin Glazer, coauthor of the screenplay. A Paramount story editor, Glazer originally bought *Tortilla Flat* for $4,000. When he left that studio several years later, he obtained the rights for about the same price; after the success of *The Grapes of Wrath*, he sold them to MGM for $90,000 (if Steinbeck's version of the story can be believed).[6] In any case Glazer made a good thing of the deal, and he was the person most interested in the production of the film. However, his screenwriting credits indicate no great talent for adapting literary properties; nor do the credits of co-screenwriter John Lee Mahin, who scripted such popular fantasies as *Show Boat* (1951) and *The Bad Seed* (1956). And it is the screenplay with its gross oversimplification of the novel that must bear a good deal of the blame for the film's failure. In fact, the final third of the film is entirely outside Steinbeck's intentions in his novel.[7]

In addition, though the cast contains a number of excellent professionals none of them get very close to the characters they are portraying. This is nowhere more strongly evident than in the variety of accents they adopt. Spencer Tracy seems to be trying the hardest to capture the lyrical, ironic, slightly archaic rhythms of Steinbeck's Pilon, but even his reading becomes faintly ridiculous, a transposition of his Portuguese seaman from *Captains Courageous* (1937) (which was also directed by Victor Fleming). John Garfield offers a Danny straight out of New York's Lower East Side, and as Sweets Ramirez, the love of his life, Hedy Lamar manages to suggest that the Flat was part of the Austro-Hungarian Empire. This confusion of international accents is compounded by Akim Tamiroff, whose Pablo seems more a Slavic peasant than a *paisano*. The rest of the characters spout "movie Mexican," only a cut up from the Cisco Kid, or they attempt no accent at all. This course works best for Frank Morgan (the actual Wizard of Oz for Fleming in 1939) as the Pirate, a sweet, simple old man. Morgan steals the show with the only performance that captures anything of the character Steinbeck created.

The film opens with the studio version of Tortilla Flat behind the credits, followed by a short on-screen narration which substitutes for Steinbeck's Preface. A few shots help establish the major characters: Danny is the romantic hero, a happy-go-lucky lover and fighter; Pilon is his mentor, the charming leader of all *paisano* ne'er-do-wells; Pablo is the third member of this central trio, a near caricature of a lazy "movie Mexican." Complicating characters are Sweets Ramirez, Danny's love interest, who tempts him to respectability, and Pirate, a simple old man who tempts Pilon to duplicity.

The story opens when an Anglo lawyer arrives in the Flat to sign over to Danny two houses bequeathed to him by his grandfather. Danny, however, is in jail for breaking windows while on a glorious drunk, and the lawyer must deal with the wily Pilon and Pablo. Pilon then guides the lawyer to the jail, where Danny at first refuses this new responsibility. Like Steinbeck's, the film's *paisanos*, prove anything but materialistic; they simply don't comprehend the acquisitive spirit of American culture, as the lawyer points out. After the lawyer leaves, Pilon appropriates a watch belonging to Danny's grandfather, by convincing Danny that he has no need for the time in jail. Close-ups project the watch as a symbol of the system they reject. Pilon trades it for three gallons of wine, and persuades the jailer to release Danny so that he can inspect his new properties. On the way up the hill to the Flat, Danny encounters Sweets Ramirez, newly arrived from Salinas, and the sparks of love start to fly in some obvious two-shots. When the *paisanos* arrive at one new house to drink away the evening the introductions are finished.

The second major sequence, like the introduction, follows Steinbeck's story fairly closely but oversimplifies his characters. It depicts the founding of the Round Table, though no hint of the Arthurian parallels is given in the movie. A housewarming party celebrates the good fortune of Danny and his *paisano* comrades. Pilon then "rents" the second house, "subletting" to Pablo, but this duplication is soon disposed of when they burn it down during the second housewarming. Danny is unconcerned, as he is consumed with love for Sweets, who seems cool to his charms. To console him, the friends settle into his house, the Camelot of Tortilla Flat.

The *paisano* "knights" perform their first good deed by aiding the Mexican father of a young baby, an incident considerably softened from the book. Next they help feed a fatherless family, a scene that reeks of condescension to Chicanos who are shown as being compounded of tortillas and beans. The friends begin a "Grand" quest when Pirate joins them and enlists their aid in carrying out his vow to supply a golden candlestick for St. Francis of Assisi's altar. Pirate's story provides a good example of how the movie softens the novel's ironies. In both movie and book, Pirate makes his vow to St. Francis to save the life of one of his sick pups. In the novel he mentions that the dog was later run over by a truck; in the movie the little dog is right up there, on the screen, wagging his tail in close-up.

Pirate becomes a sort of *paisano* St. Francis of Assisi himself. The whole Pirate episode is so extended and sentimentalized that it threatens to take over the movie and is closer in spirit to *Lassie Comes Home* (1943) than to Steinbeck's novel. Frank Morgan delivers several soliloquies to St. Francis in close-up while soft light beams down on him from the heavens. When he finally achieves his quest, the scene at the church resembles something out of *The Song of Bernadette* (1944). While this sort of pseudo-piety was common in the films of that day, it was miles away from Steinbeck's ironic intentions.

The film also sanitizes Danny's relationship with Sweets, the other major plot complication. In the novel, "her voice was shrill, her face hard and sharp as a hatchet, her figure lumpy, and her intentions selfish" (154)[8]; she is only softened when the yen for a man overcomes her about once a week, hence her ironic nickname. In the movie, the sweet side predominates over Latin temper in the person of the meltingly beautiful and far from "lumpy" Hedy Lamarr. Steinbeck's Danny courts her with the gift of a broken vacuum cleaner, but his friends soon rescue him from the snares of domesticity. Hollywood's Danny pursues her single-mindedly, trading his guitar for the vacuum cleaner, and he even takes a job to provide her with electricity. He hopes some day to buy his own fishing boat and then propose marriage to Sweets.

As in the novel, Pilon interferes, tricking Danny into an angry confrontation with Sweets at the cannery in which she works. (The cannery seems location shot, the only realistic setting in the film.) When the manager tries to throw him out, Danny fights, falls, and strikes his head on a machine. Hospitalized, in a coma, Danny hovers at death's door, while all his friends pray for him at St. Francis' altar. The cynical Pilon—suffused with movie light—even promises another gold candlestick to St. Francis in return for Danny's life. In good happy ending fashion, Danny recovers, is reconciled with Pilon, and marries Sweets. The thoughtful pastor has converted the candlestick into a fishing boat so Danny and Sweets are left to live happily in Tortilla Flat, blessedly elevated to middle-class entrepreneurship. Danny's house burns down accidently, and the other *paisanos* happily return to sleeping on the beach in the final scene, a reprise of the opening shots of Pilon and Pablo.

In Steinbeck's novel, the little Camelot of Tortilla Flat ends more tragically. Danny goes mad, turns on his friends at a party given to cheer him up, rushes outside to find an imaginary opponent waiting for him, and falls to his death from a cliff. Then the *paisanos* burn the house, as though it were the pyre of some ancient hero. This heavy conclusion, arbitrarily transposed from Malory's *Morte d'Arthur*, does not really arise out of Steinbeck's story, however, and it presents almost as many problems as the studio version.

The happy wedding merely provides the culminating Hollywood touch to the film's sentimentalizing of all the people and events in Steinbeck's book. But in 1942 World War II was providing Americans with enough reality and complexity; most reviewers praised the film as solid entertainment. For example, the nameless *Newsweek* reviewer, in a notable misunderstanding of modes, opens by saying, "Probably nothing short of a documentary film . . . could hope to capture the earthy and amoral spirit of John Steinbeck's *Tortilla Flat* . . . the film is a reasonable facsimile."[10] From today's perspective it seems a rather unreasonable sepia-toned sham that could have only been made in Hollywood.

III. THE MOON IS DOWN

Steinbeck's first novel since *The Grapes of Wrath*, *The Moon Is Down*, was published in February 1942; a dramatic version opened on Broadway in April of that year; and the film version appeared in March 1943. Obviously anticipating a stage version and a screen adaptation, Steinbeck had written the novel in the dramatic form he employed in *Of Mice and Men*. Although novel, play, and film received mixed reviews, all three versions proved popular with the general public. The work earned Steinbeck a great deal of money, but he seemed to realize that it represented a falling off of his talents, particularly in terms of direct observation.[1] *The Moon Is Down* fails artistically in all three mediums because they break with the nonteleological thinking behind his best work and present melodramatic versions of what totalitarian occupation might be like.

This failure of observation is nowhere more evident than in the choice of setting. Steinbeck began the work early in 1941 as a speculative account of the possible invasion of California; the coastal town clearly was modeled on Monterey.[2] As America moved toward war, Steinbeck revised the work, and the setting came to resemble occupied Europe. As eventually published, the novel is set in an allegorical "never-never land." This compromise was bad for Steinbeck's purposes, as his best work had always been rooted in his native land, and when he moved away from it he tended to get lost in sentiment and melodrama. Unrooted in the reality of place, his characters in *The Moon Is Down* become types who act out the writer's themes in a plot so mechanically predetermined that its development can be foreseen in the first chapter. Like *Bombs Away!*, *The Moon Is Down* is better as propaganda than literature. Steinbeck tells us his theme is "the durability of democracy."[3] As one character puts it: "it is always the herd men who win battles, and the free men who win wars."(186)[4] The characters, the events, the settings are created to demonstrate this theory without regard for motivation, credibility, or realism. These problems did not escape some reviewers, though surprisingly they were much more critical of Steinbeck's portrayal of the Nazis as human at all.

The propagandistic emphasis in both the novel and the

play versions of *The Moon Is Down* is escalated in the film adaptation. Enthused by the book's "message," Twentieth Century-Fox had outbid several studios for the film rights. Nunnally Johnson, the screenwriter of *The Grapes of Wrath*, was assigned as producer, and he wrote his own screenplay after consultation with Steinbeck. The author encouraged the screenwriter to make whatever changes he wished, evidently trusting Johnson's artistic judgment after his work on *The Grapes of Wrath*. As indicated in the discussion of the earlier film, Johnson was a competent Hollywood professional capable of entertaining, clear, and "sincere" adaptations of literary properties, but the man who had been unequal to the complexities of *The Grapes of Wrath* was not the one to improve on the simplifications of *The Moon Is Down*. When Steinbeck saw the film, he wrote to Johnson: "There is no question that pictures are a better medium for this story than the stage ever was."[5] He seems to approve of the film's propaganda—another indication of how his ideas had changed with the war.

In many ways screenwriter-producer Johnson seems more the *auteur* of *The Moon Is Down* on the screen, than either the novelist or the director, Irving Pichel. Steinbeck found his own dramatic version "dull,"[6] and he told Johnson "to tamper with it."[7] Johnson opened up the work, much as Lewis Milestone had done with the tight dramatic structure in *Of Mice and Men*. Avoiding the two-room set of the play, Johnson naturally uses the whole village as his scene. Although this allows him to dramatize offstage events, these changes only increase the tendency toward melodrama, making the enemy more the stock heavies of war movies and the homefolks more the traditional good guys. Nor do the changes increase the visual realism of the film. This European village had just served as a Welsh coal-mining town for John Ford's *How Green Was My Valley* (1943), and the studio look calls attention to itself[8] as Johnson locates his story in Norway.

The rest of the production company also contribute to Johnson's stolid conception of the work. A sometime actor, Irving Pichel was essentially a studio hack best known as a director for campy action—*The Most Dangerous Game* (1932), *She* (1935), *Destination Moon* (1950)—or sentimental melodrama—*A Medal for Benny* (1945) (also from a Steinbeck story), *The Miracle of the Bells* (1948). Pichel probably exaggerated the worst aspects of Johnson's script, while he added little in terms of visual realization. Cameraman Arthur Miller had done much better work; for the most part *The Moon Is Down* has a glossy studio glow and absolutely wooden movement.

The cast further stylizes the screenplay's characterizations. Sir Cedric Hardwicke transforms Steinbeck's Colonel Lanser into a typical screen Nazi, while Henry Travers completely sentimentalizes the role of Mayor Orden. Most of the supporting roles are similarly simplified, especially Dorris Bowden (Mrs. Nunnally Johnson) as Molly Morden, Margaret Wycherly as Madame Orden, E. J. Ballantine as the Quisling, George Corell, and director Pichel himself as Peder. More interesting performances are provided by a youthful Lee J. Cobb as thoughtful Dr. Winter and Peter Van Eyck as Lieutenant Tonder, a squeamish enemy officer whose "sensitivity" sets him at odds with his countrymen.

After the credits, which are backed by rather dramatic music, the film opens with the attack on the peaceful village by the enemy forces. Steinbeck had the fighting discussed only after the fact, but the movie presents it, emphasizing and exaggerating the betrayal of the tiny home defense force by the traitor George Corell. As in the novel and play, Corell's role is ambiguous, and it is never made clear if he is a sort of Norwegian Quisling or an enemy spy. In any case, he facilitates the capture of the town by the enemy, and Mayor Orden prepares to receive their commander. As in Steinbeck's version the Mayor's living room becomes the headquarters of the occupation forces, and the room is transformed from a pleasant, homey living place into an armed camp. Much as in the novel, the enemy officers are introduced as they settle into their new quarters, though the cast of characters is somewhat reduced.

Most important is the commander, Lanser, whose name indicates his military character. A professional soldier and World War I veteran, Lanser knows the futility of this invasion. Steinbeck's Lanser, humanized but unmotivated, is something of an enigma. The film solves this problem by having Sir Cedric Hardwicke play the colonel as a cold, cynical, self-serving type. The complexity of young Tonder, the "poetic" soul, is preserved in the film, and his death later becomes the best realized sequence in it.

The first third of the movie, serves as an introduction. The invasion takes place, and the occupation forces set up a routine for the local coal mine. The townspeople are too stunned to react. In the second part of the film, resistance to the invaders stiffens. Despite Corell's assurances that the local population is too timid and weak for resistance, acts of sabotage become common. This resistance is presented both in general, through the use of montage, and in particular, by a complicated plot strand involving Alex Morden (William Post, Jr.) a hot-tempered miner, who when abused by an enemy officer kills his foe with his pickax. Again Johnson and Pichel dramatize action which takes place off stage in the earlier versions. The miner is sentenced by a military court and executed by a firing squad under the command of the young Tonder. The execution prepares for mass slaughter later in the film, and it also involves Tonder with Molly Morden (Doris Bowden), the miner's widow. When the guilt-ridden young officer visits her, offering his help, she invites him back for what he assumes will be a tryst. Instead she stabs him to death in forceful scene presented on camera, though in the play this scene is only suggested.

Tonder's death indicates the hardening of resistance into a murderous resolve. When occupiers are picked off by phantom snipers, Lanser orders a half-dozen miners to be randomly chosen for execution. In these scenes, created for the film from the slightest suggestion in Steinbeck's versions, the movie resembles many other Hollywood representations of Nazi occupied nations. The men go to their deaths singing the national anthem, and when the burst of enemy weapons silences them, the whole village picks up the song in an act of mass defiance.

From here on it is open warfare with weapons and dynamite smuggled in from England. The film, like the novel and play, ends when Mayor Orden is taken as a hostage whose life will be forfeited if resistance continues. The acts of sabotage continue, and he goes to his death after a philosophical debate with Colonel Lanser in which Orden asserts that "the little people won't go under." An officious little man at the film's opening, the mayor goes to his death with dignity, repeating Socrates' final words to Crito in the *Phaedo:* "Crito, I owe a cock to Asclepius. Will you remember to pay the debt?" His friend, Dr. Winter (Lee J. Cobb) answers in the words of Crito: "The debt will be paid." His answer indicates that the resistance will go on until the townsfolk are free once more. Mayor Orden becomes the symbol of the Western heritage which the Nazis would destroy, and his sacrifice proclaims the futility of their purpose. His words like those of Socrates are meant to live in the memory of free men.

Viewed from today's perspective the film is interesting as an indication of America's, Hollywood's, and Steinbeck's attitudes in the early years of World War II. As a literary, dramatic, and filmic work, *The Moon Is Down* suffers from unrealistic settings, characters, and events. Like both the novel and the play, the film was taken to task for its *ersatz* setting, its good guy-bad guy characterization, and its melodramatic confrontations. James Agee, writing in *The Nation*, complained that it added to "the growing, already overripe vocabulary of democratic claptrap which all but destroys our realization that modest heroism is constant, possible, and implicit in this war."[9] However, more typical of the general reaction was that of *New York Times* critic Bosley Crowther who lauded the film for avoiding the problems of the novel and the play. He praised Nunnally Johnson's screenplay because it "wrung out any traces of defeatism" present in the earlier version by giving more definition to the theme—"that the will of a free and noble people cannot be suppressed by violence."[10] The critics for *Time* and *Newsweek* also found the film much stronger than the earlier versions.

Quite obviously, in 1943 America wanted not art but propaganda, and Hollywood was ready to provide it. Even Steinbeck's comparatively unemotional patriotism did not fit the mood of the country. Not complex, penetrating analysis of the world at war, but only reassuring, patriotic melodrama was the order of the day.

A comparison of *The Moon Is Down* in all its versions, with two other Hollywood features concerned with occupied Norway is instructive. John Farrow directed Paul Muni and Sir Cedric Hardwicke (this time as a British officer) in *The Commandos Strike at Dawn* (1942), with a screenplay by novelist Irwin Shaw from a story by C. S. Forester, the creator of *Captain Horatio Hornblower*. Even Bosley Crowther had a hard time with this one in which commandos sweep "to the rescue in good old United States Cavalry style."[11] *Edge of Darkness* (1943), with screenplay by Robert Rossen from William Woods's novel of the same title, starred Errol Flynn as the leader of the resistance. It was directed by Lewis Milestone, who was not only the creator of the realistic *Of Mice and Men*, but of *All Quiet on the Western Front* (1930), Hollywood's most notable antiwar film. In *Edge of Darkness* a group of hostages, including Flynn and heroine Ann Sheridan, are about to be executed when the local pastor, pretending to bless them, whips out a machine gun and mows the firing squad down. Flynn, Sheridan, and the good paster (earlier a pacifist) then lead the villagers in a bloody rout of the Nazis.

(Interestingly enough, *Edge of Darkness* was shot in Monterey, the nearest equivalent to Norway Milestone could find.) Even the British documentary *Commandos* (1943), reduces a raid to little more than an adventure story. In this context, what are now seen as the excesses by both Nunnally Johnson and John Steinbeck seem understandable. Unfortunately Steinbeck's literary and cinematic work of the postwar years, continued in a similar vein.

IV. LIFEBOAT

Critical complaints against Steinbeck's next film, *Lifeboat* (1944), exactly contradicted the reaction to *The Moon Is Down*. The earlier work elicited ire because it was thought soft on the Nazis, depicting them as subject to human hesitations and weaknesses. *Lifeboat* was attacked for portraying its Nazi villain as too strong, for perpetuating Hitler's myth of the Aryan superman. Such charges now appear as an unwarranted product of wartime hysteria and superpatriotism. Nevertheless, the film can be faulted for its simplistic allegory, its glossy Hollywood photography, and its high melodrama. Despite the collaboration of a great writer and of a great director—Alfred Hitchcock—*Lifeboat* remains an interesting failure.

The major problem with it is perhaps the confusion of multiple authorship. Hitchcock seems the most unlikely of directors to capture Steinbeck for the screen; the themes, subjects, and style of the two artists are almost diametrically opposite. In the case of *Lifeboat*, the *auteurship* problem is further muddled by the work of other screenwriters. When the complications of a Hollywood wartime production were added to the conflicting visions of the two primary *auteurs*, the result is a curious hodgepodge, interesting primarily for its relationship to the more successful works of the writer and the director. Although most literary and film critics have dismissed *Lifeboat*, blaming its artistic failure on one or the other *auteur* or the wartime production atmosphere, despite its failings *Lifeboat* is actually a significant work in the careers of both artists.

Steinbeck wrote a "novelette," not a screenplay, for the production of *Lifeboat*.[1] The revised version of his story treatment runs to about 40,000 words, a fairly substantial work not much shorter than *The Moon Is Down* or *Bombs Away!* Steinbeck's *Lifeboat* proves a combination of these two wartime works, and a stronger literary effort than can be inferred from the film version. Since the original treatment has never been published, most Steinbeck critics have failed to appreciate the importance of the work in the development of the writer's career. *Lifeboat* not only builds on earlier work, but it suggests what Steinbeck might have done if he had continued to develop in the directions indicated in this wartime work. *Lifeboat* has the makings of a good war novel, though, like the film, it is finally sunk by the allegorical freight with which Steinbeck loads his little craft. Nevertheless, the story treatment indicates that Steinbeck might well have fashioned fine fiction from the factual materials of his later war dispatches. Unfortunately, he was to turn back to the weakest of his California materials, the sentimentalized underdogs of Monterey, and his next novel, *Cannery Row* (1945), was a reprise of *Tortilla Flat*.

Steinbeck took the *Lifeboat* assignment in much the same spirit that went into *Bombs Away!*. Late in 1942 the Merchant Marine asked Hollywood to make a propaganda piece on the vital convoys that plied the North Atlantic in the face of German submarine attacks. They contacted Darryl Zanuck the producer of *The Grapes of Wrath*, who in turn asked Steinbeck to do a screenplay.[2] Steinbeck, who was waiting for assignment overseas, agreed to do a story treatment for which the studio would pay only if they made use of it. This was his first assignment for Hollywood, and his second effort, after *The Forgotten Village*, at writing directly for the film medium.

The final story treatment, dated March 26, 1943, indicates that Steinbeck approached the movie much as he had the earlier documentary. First he did his research, including interviews with seaman survivors of torpedo attacks.[3] He took a small group and turned them into a microcosm of American society, but though the characters are symbolic, their development is realistic. In *The Grapes of Wrath*, Steinbeck successfully balanced realism and symbolic purpose; in *The Forgotten Village* he did not quite maintain that balance. The problem with *Lifeboat* is that it fails to balance the conflicting tensions. Nevertheless Steinbeck's "novelette" does achieve this balance much better than the film. This is because his treatment was considerably more realistic and documentary than what finally reached the screen.

Steinbeck tells the story from the first-person viewpoint of Bud, a young merchant seaman. This precisely defined viewpoint enhances realism by making Bud the source of observation about the Merchant Marine as well as of the other characters. Bud is a down-to-earth working man, a sort of Tom Joad gone to sea, who knows his job and does it well. His narration is straightforward and realistic, and Steinbeck underlines this aspect in several places by comparison to documentary photography. For example, when Bud's ship is torpedoed, he recalls the scene in these terms: "In my mind I get a picture that was all in slow motion; everything was a kind of newsreel color, . . . the figures of the people were black and the air around them was a kind of newsreel gray."[4] The same imagery is also used in his description of the sea battle that ends the story. The details of life both aboard the ship and in the boat are much more realistically handled in Steinbeck's "novelette" than in the final film. Even more importantly, though the characters are typed to some extent, they are not the stock melodramatic types of the movie.

   Since Steinbeck's story received several reworkings before it appeared as a film, blame is difficult to access.[5] In an
interview Hitchcock describes the evolution of the script:

> I had assigned John Steinbeck to the screenplay, but
> his treatment was incomplete and so I brought in MacKin-
> lay Kantor, who worked on it for two weeks. I didn't care for
> what he had written at all. He said, "Well, that's the best I
> can do." I thanked him for his efforts and hired another
> writer, Jo Swerling, who had worked on several films for
> Frank Capra. When the screenplay was completed and I was
> ready to shoot, I discovered that the narrative was rather
> shapeless. So I went over it again, trying to give a dramatic
> form to each of the sequences.[6]

With each rewriting Steinbeck's story was changed: Kantor
heightened the allegory; Swerling provided Hollywood gloss;
and Hitchcock created a thriller.
   The problems are evident from the opening shot in which
the credits are projected over the image of a freighter's
smokestack sinking into troubled waters. The sea is rather
obviously a studio tank, and the tank provides the setting of
the entire film. Changes in weather are created with wind
machines and rear-projection backdrops. Although the technical effects by Hollywood veteran Fred Sersen are very good,
they never create the sense of documentary realism necessary
to balance the central allegory. Instead the *ersatz* ocean
visually replicates the literary cliché of desperate people
thrown together by fate in a lifeboat that becomes a sort of
sea-going *Stagecoach* (1939) or *Grand Hotel* (1932).
   The personalities of the characters prove even more
bewildering than their suspiciously impeccable Hollywood
grooming after weeks at sea. Steinbeck had created types, but
not stereotypes. His cast included Bud, the salt-of-the-earth
seaman; Albert, a tough Polish stoker from the Chicago
stockyards; Joe, a thoughtful black man who had been the
steward on board; Brennan, a self-made millionaire; Connie

Porter, a former actress became a Congresswoman; Lt. Both, an army nurse; a nameless English woman and her infant child; a Nazi seaman, a survivor of the submarine which was sung in the battle with the freighter. Obviously, the group was chosen to represent a variety of responses to a world at war. Hitchcock retained all these characters—though he renamed several—and he added another: Stanley Garret or Sparks, a British radioman. Garrett (played by Hume Cronyn) was probably intended to stress the joint Anglo-American war effort.

In Hitchcock's grouping, the most important character becomes not Bud but Connie Porter, now a brassy newswoman played by Tallulah Bankhead. Miss Bankhead was a notable stage personality who made a few films in the early days of sound and then returned to the legitimate theater until Hitchcock tempted her with a hefty offer for the film. Perversely cast against type, Miss Bankhead turns in a performance that overshadows the others and unfortunately gives Mrs. Porter a prominence out of proportion with her place in the allegory. Bud—Steinbeck's central figure—is rebaptized Gus by the screenwriters and becomes the stereotype of the jiving sailor boy familiar from World War II navy movies.[7] Other characters also get name and personality changes. Not only does Albert the stoker become Kovac, but his character becomes essentially simpler as interpreted by John Hodiak. The same simplification is true of Brennan, who for some reason becomes Rittenhouse, played broadly by veteran Henry Hill. Joe picks up the nickname "Charcoal," and generally is reduced to the stereotyped screen black of the period despite the sensitivity Canada Lee brings to the role. Nurse Both becomes Alice Mackenzie, and as she is played by Mary Anderson the characterization remains similar. The deranged English woman is named Mrs. Higgins, and she is capably recreated by Heather Angel.

The most important character change is in the Nazi seaman, who acquires the name Willy and the rank of

Captain. These changes reflect his transformation in Walter Slezak's melodramatic, almost campy performance. Steinbeck's Nazi was a type, but a human type, much like the characters he created in *The Moon Is Down*. Hitchcock's *Lifeboat*, like the movie version of the earlier work, presents a screen Nazi more acceptable to wartime audiences. However, under Hitchcock's direction Slezak's Willy becomes something of a droll superman. Hitchcock was given to archvillains who present a charming, smiling surface. His film just previous to *Lifeboat, Shadow of Doubt* (1943) presents an excellent example in the Bluebeard murderer, Uncle Charlie, suavely played by Joseph Cotton. In addition, Hitchcock obviously enjoyed the thrills of a plot which pitted an evil mastermind against good but weak people, who as they unravel a complex mystery are forced to face up to some of life's dark complexities; the central conflict of the screen *Lifeboat* becomes Hitchcock's not Steinbeck's version of the struggle begeen good and evil.

Events are also changed considerably from "novelette" to film. Steinbeck begins his version before the sinking of the freighter, allowing for considerable documentary detail concerned with life in the Merchant Marine. The pages which present this material and document the sea battle are the best in the work, and they indicate what Steinbeck might have done with the war story. This material was cut by Hitchcock, perhaps justifiably in terms of time.

Instead, the movie opens with the image of the sinking, followed by a pan of the debris-strewn sea, replete with a Hitchcockian ironic touch—a *New Yorker* magazine floating near a dead Nazi submariner. Hitchcock also alters the order of the characters arrival in the solitary drifting lifeboat. Connie Porter, already in the boat when the camera picks it up, provides Bankhead with a characteristically dramatic entrance, which establishes her as the central character. Busy photographing the wreckage, she sees Kovac swimming to the craft through her viewfinder but does not help him aboard until she has taken the picture. His arrival sparks an argument which indicates a clash between the characters soon made more evident when he knocks her camera overboard. The others are then picked up in approximately the order of the story. When Willy arrives a pair of hands suddenly appear over the side of the boat, and a monstrous creature looms up from the sea—filling the frame like the Creature from the Black Lagoon.

As in the story, the group (representing the Allied Powers) debate what course to take with Willy (Hitler, the Nazis, Germany). Kovac wants to toss him back into the sea, but others want to save him for humanitarian (Alice) or pragmatic reasons (Rittenhouse). After all, he is a fellow human being lost at sea—*and* he can navigate. In a vote, the majority elect to keep him on board.

During the debate Steinbeck's analysis of the political shift from the 1930s to the 1940s is reduced to a few hot phrases between Kovac the Socialist and Rittenhouse the Capitalist. After settling this issue, the occupants of the boat argue about their course of action. Like the democracies they are disoriented by events, as is shown by the fact that they literally don't know which way to steer. Another vote is taken, and Rittenhouse is elected Captain. Almost immediately he comes under the influence of the Nazi, the submarine *Kommandant*. Steinbeck and Hitchcock both seem to imply the danger of using totalitarian means to achieve democratic ends, an obvious problem for a democracy at war. The tensions thus established persist throughout the picture, becoming the most important dramatic element.

The action is punctuated by a number of dramatic events. The English woman's baby dies, and, when they separate her from it, she becomes despondent and disappears over the side during the survivors' first night. Then the next several days engage the group in pleasant activity—singing, cardplaying, flirting—all shown in dull two- and three-shot setups. Meanwhile Willy plots a course with a hidden compass, which is given symbolic value by tight close-up. The villain is able to ingratiate himself with the group when he amputates Gus's gangrenous leg—it seems Super Willy is also a surgeon. Again overly dramatic close-ups of the knife alternate with static set pieces of the group gathered around poor Gus. (Of course, none of these events occurred in Steinbeck's original; they were suggested by a slight leg wound Bud received in the sinking of his ship.) Willy is now plotting to steer them away from land, evidently to a rendezvous with a German supply ship. Sparks (not Bud as in the story) realizes that something strange is going on, but the resulting debate over what course to take is cut short by a violent storm.

In the storm they lose all their supplies and more importantly most of their water. Under the circumstances, Willy becomes the real Captain of the craft. Having secretly kept back some of the water, he is the only one strong enough to row the boat, and row on he does—singlehandedly. Of course, this is patently ridiculous, as one man could not propel a boat of this size, and the straight shots of Willy rowing away while singing German *lieder* are ludicrous. As the others weaken, they comfort each other; romance blossoms between Kovac and Connie, as well as between Sparks and the nurse. (In the story Albert woos the nurse, while Connie and millionaire Brenner get together.) Meanwhile Joe sings "Negro" spirituals; Rittenhouse snivels, and Gus begins to hallucinate. It is Gus who finds out that the Nazi has an unshared water supply; as a result, Willy is forced to toss him overboard while the others sleep, a piece of arch-villainy. Sparks suspects the truth, and when they finally search Willy they also find food tablets, compass, knife, etc.

The most interesting scene in the film follows when the rest of the group turn on Willy in a rage. Only Joe, the black, holds back as the others vent their frustration on the Nazi; when Willy clings to the gunwale, in close-up Rittenhouse smashes his hands with Gus's old boot until he slips into the sea. In an interview, Hitchcock likened their behavior to "a pack of dogs,"[8] a judgment confirmed by the mass of their backs and the slight down angle in the shot. Yet Hitchcock refrained from confirming François Truffaut's hypothesis that the scene shows that all of people became beasts in the war.[9] However, this reading seems substantiated by many other Hitchcock films which indicate that pervasive evil infects even the best of characters. Good examples are the ending of *Shadow of a Doubt* (1943), where the "good" girl has been affected by her evil Uncle Charlie, or the ghastly kitchen murder in the Cold War thriller, *Torn Curtain* (1966).

In any case, stung by Joe's accusation of mob behavior, the characters debate their guilt. Finally Connie absolves them of the charge by pointing out the extreme provocation, rallies their strength by cleverly fishing for food with her diamond pin, and inspires them to row on. However, they have gone too far on Willy's course, and they are intercepted by the German supply ship—a typically ironic Hitchcock ending.

At this point, the Hollywood script takes over as an American destroyer in turn sinks the Nazi ship. After the battle, as the occupants of the boat await final rescue, another pair of hands appear over the side of the boat in close-up. Soon another representative of the Master Race is hauled in—this time a frightened boy. They try to help him, but like Willy he proves treacherous, pulling a concealed pistol. Joe disarms him easily enough, and another execution debate ensues. Finally Kovac asks: "What are you going to do with people like that?" Like the rest of the world, the group has no answer.

Lifeboat is a rather obvious allegory of the world situation in 1944, and though Steinbeck intended the allegory, he at least partially balanced it with a realistic depiction of setting, character, and event. This compensating realism is lost in the film's overlay of Hollywood gloss and Hitchcockian high intrigue.[10]

Steinbeck, who evidently failed to realize what the original "novelette" might have meant for him, nevertheless blamed Hitchcock for the artistic failure of the film. In a private letter he said,

> It does not seem right that knowing the effect of the picture on many people, the studio still lets it go. As for Hitchcock, I think his reasons were very simple. He has been doing stories of international spies and master minds for so long that it has become a habit. And second, he is one of those incredible English middle class snobs who really and truly despise working people. As you know, there were other things that bothered me—technical things. I know that one man can't row a boat of that size and in my story, no one touched an oar except to steer.[11]

He complained to the studio about the characterization of Kovac—"an intelligent and thoughtful seaman" in his version—and Joe—"a Negro of dignity reduced to the usual colored travesty."[12] Later, in a telegram to his agent he stated:

> PLEASE CONVEY THE FOLLOWING TO 20TH CENTURY FOX: IN VIEW OF THE FACT THAT MY SCRIPT FOR THE PICTURE *LIFEBOAT* WAS DISTORTED IN PRODUCTION SO THAT ITS LINE AND INTENTION HAS BEEN CHANGED AND BECAUSE THE PICTURE SEEMS TO ME TO BE DANGEROUS TO THE AMERICAN WAR EFFORT I REQUEST MY NAME BE REMOVED FROM ANY CONNECTION WITH ANY SHOWING OF THIS FILM.
> JOHN STEINBECK[13]

Whether or not *Lifeboat* was dangerous to the American war effort, it was certainly detrimental to John Steinbeck's career as a writer; his later work was closer to the movie than to his own short novel which engendered it.[14]

V. A MEDAL FOR BENNY

Steinbeck's final film of the war years, *A Medal for Benny* (1945), foreshadows the decline of his talents in the years to come. Like his novel of the same year, *Cannery Row*, the movie simultaneously looks backward to his easy success in *Tortilla Flat* and forward to his close involvement with screenwriting in sentimental pieces like *The Red Pony* (1949).

A Medal for Benny is based on an unpublished story by Steinbeck and Jack Wagner, a boyhood friend who with his brother, Max Wagner, went to Hollywood to work at a variety of film jobs. (It was the Wagners who introduced Steinbeck to his second wife, Gwen Conger.) Jack's only screenwriting credit to date was *The Dancing Pirate* (1936), but the commercial success of *Tortilla Flat* in 1942 indicated to him that there would be an easy market for a sequel, and Steinbeck was willing to give the venture a try. Over the years his literary collaboration changed from his scientific study with Ed Ricketts to Hollywood hackwork with Jack Wagner.

The coauthors quickly tricked up a story during the months the novelist was waiting for overseas assignment, and Steinbeck's agent sold it to Paramount for $25,000.[1] The studio assigned veteran screenwriter Frank Butler to develop a screenplay from the story with Wagner's assistance.[2] Although Butler's screenplay has been published, the original story is not available, and it is therefore not quite fair to blame Steinbeck for the ensuing mess.[3] Yet he had created the original *paisano* material, and he countenanced the final product. As with *Lifeboat*, he objected, but this time not so vigorously.[4] Wagner and Butler were undoubtedly responsible for the more egregious clichés, but Steinbeck's touches are evident in much of the movie.

Butler was a studio journeyman, responsible for efforts like *Waikiki Wedding* (1937) followed by *Paris Honeymoon* (1938), as well as several of the Bing Crosby-Bob Hope *Road* series. During the war years, he wrote the superpatriotic *Wake Island* (1942) and the supersentimental *Going My Way* (1943), in which Bing Crosby and Barry Fitzgerald spread pastoral charm in a poor Catholic parish. Thus, it is more than likely that the hyped-up patriotism and sentimentality of *A Medal for Benny* largely derive from him. Irving Pichel, who also directed *The Moon Is Down*, employs the same wooden, clichéd pictorial style which marked his film version of that earlier Steinbeck work. The cast was made up of essentially supporting players, who were here elevated to feature roles. Their unsubtle and sentimental performances only served to emphasize the flaws in Steinbeck's original conception and the distortion of his characters. Overall, the production is glossy and false in the worst Hollywood style of the period.

Steinbeck is responsible for the central subject matter, Tortilla Flat at War, and for the major plot strand, the transformation of Charley Martini. The return to the easy materials of *Tortilla Flat*, his first instance of literary backtracking, was bad enough, but he compounded the error by enlisting his *paisanos* in the war effort. The whole point of his earlier book was to suggest the superiority of the *paisanos'* easygoing life-styles to middle-class American virtues. In Steinbeck's book Danny, Pilon, and Big Joe Portagee had joined the Army in World War I, but they were drunk at the moment of their enlistment and eventually spent most of their time in the stockade. *A Medal for Benny* shows the knockabout *paisanos* becoming patriotic and efficient warriors, worthy of the highest military honors. Steinbeck seems to have been inspired by the movie version of *Tortilla Flat* rather than his own 1935 novel. That movie's unconvincing conversion of Danny and Pilon to middle-class sobriety is in *A Medal for Benny* repeated in the persons of Benny, Charley Martini, and Joe Morales.

In an interesting strategy, Steinbeck's title character never appears in the movie. Evidently a wildman in the mold of the earlier Danny, Benny has been run out of town by the police. Although he has completely disappeared, his improvident father, Charley, still expects his boy to return a success and save him from a life of poverty. Charley is portrayed by veteran supporting actor J. Caroll Naish in what is the film's best performance, though it is true that the competition is small. (Naish's best performance of a long career was as a tenant farmer in his next film, *The Southerner*, directed that same year by Jean Renoir from a screenplay by William Faulkner.) His role here is basically unbelievable; Charley's only function is to advance Steinbeck's theme of the simple good life of the *paisanos*.

When the film opens Charley is about to be evicted from his house because he cannot meet the bank payments. As evidence of his good faith, he takes his real property— chickens, goats, dogs, etc.—to the bank and inevitably a wild scene ensues when all this barnyard life runs amuck. Later Charley thinks that the Anglos who come to the house intend to serve him eviction papers, but instead they announce that his son, the long lost Benny, has died a hero's death in the defense of the Philippines—taking over a hundred Japanese with him. The governor and a general personally intend to present Charley with Benny's posthumous Medal of Honor, and since the Chamber of Commerce types do not want the visiting dignitaries to see Tortilla Flat, they install Charley in a beautiful new home in the Anglo suburbs. Chaos ensues when Charley starts selling off the furnishings. The mayor (played by Grant Mitchell, the FDR look-alike who ran the government camp in *The Grapes of Wrath*) is forced to confess the reason for Charley's sudden transfer to a new environment. In dignified anger, the old man deserts his new quarters and returns to the Flat, thus forcing his VIP visitors to seek him out there.

Taken by itself, this central plot development is rather obvious and more than a little corny, but it does possess some real humor and insight into middle-class hypocrisy. Unfortunately, the other writers assigned to the project provided Benny with a girl friend, Lolita Sierra, played by Dorothy Lamour. Changing from her sarongs of the Crosby-Hope *Road* movies did not improve Dottie's acting ability, and her performance makes Hedy Lamarr's Sweets Ramirez in *Tortilla Flat* look sophisticated by comparison. Mexican actor Arturo de Cordova plays opposite her as Joe Morales, Lolita's love interest and Benny's great rival. Every cliché in the

Hollywood book is employed in the courtship plot, from the demon little brother who must be bribed off to the catfight between women when Lolita finally gets jealous of Joe's attentions to another Latin bombshell. To top it all off, the screenwriters shamelessly tack on an unbelievable character transformation: in order to prove himself worthy of Lolita, Joe leaves his ne'er-do-well ways behind and joins the army. Lolita will be waiting when Joe comes marching home.

When the film appeared in May 1945, it received a mixed reception. Many critics and moviegoers obviously liked it because it provided an escape from the realities of the war. Phrases like those that described *Tortilla Flat* reappear in the reviews: "warm *paisanos* of the California coast," "colorful vagrants, amoral and full of small deceits," "impoverished, improvident, fun-loving California *paisanos*." *New York Times* reviewer Bosley Crowther thought it "a charming film,"[5] while Philip Hartung in *Commonweal* called it "a lovely little job,"[6] and even James Agee writing in *The Nation* found it "endearing."[7] Steinbeck and Wagner won an Oscar nomination for Best Original Story, as did Naish for Best Supporting Actor.

In retrospect, these effusions must be attributed to the peculiar vision of the war years. The contemporary viewer is more likely to agree with the *New Yorker's* reviewer, who pointed out that *A Medal for Benny* "utilized practically every cliché of comedy or pathos known to the screen."[8] Steinbeck was not responsible for all of these clichés, but he does have to take the blame for the ones inherent in his unlikely vision of Tortilla Flat marching off to war.

VI. THE WAR AND AFTER

Although *Lifeboat* was released in 1944 and *A Medal for Benny* in 1945, both were written before June of 1943 when Steinbeck left for the European theater of the war as special correspondent to the New York *Herald Tribune*. Steinbeck had decided to put his writing talents to work for the newspapers, when none of the armed services seemed especially interested in him.[1] Although his newly married second-wife objected, he felt a need to participate in the war effort—it was also his intention to gather material for a war novel while he documented the fighting for the press.[2]

His first dispatches were from wartorn England in July 1943; by August he had moved on to North Africa, only recently liberated by the Allies. Sicily had already been taken, and the Allied forces were poised for an invasion of the Italian mainland. In mid-September Steinbeck covered the landing of Salerno. At one point he was trapped under the heavy enemy shelling that pounded the invading forces; his eardrums burst, and he began to experience blackouts and blinding headaches. After a brief stay in England, he returned to New York in November. His European expedition had resulted in an excellent series of dispatches, which he later collected under the title *Once There Was A War* (1958). For the most part they are strong stuff, indicative of what Steinbeck might have done with this material as fiction.

Unfortunately, he did nothing with it. Perhaps stung by the criticism of *The Moon Is Down* and *Lifeboat* as inauthentic, Steinbeck fell back on more personal material for his next novel. Overwhelmed by the experience of war, he was unable to absorb and recreate it in fiction.[3] Rather than grapple with this harsh, complex subject matter, he decided to write for fun and profit. The celebrity author could enjoy life with his young wife and growing family, while he turned out pleasant best sellers. And so during 1944, while combat raged in Europe and Asia, while Hitler was marshalling the machinery for the Holocaust, while the atom bomb was being tested in the American desert, Steinbeck was writing *Cannery Row*.

The novel had been suggested to him by his publisher Pat Covici, who had visited Steinbeck in California years earlier and had recognized the commercial possibilities of a *Tortilla Flat* type of novel concerned with the colorful inhabitants of the Monterey waterfront.[4] Like the earlier book, *Cannery Row* is essentially a collection of tales united by a common setting; in this case, the stories are also connected by the desire of another band of happy-go-lucky rowdies to give a party. Mack and the "boys" may be bums to the middle class of Monterey, but they are like Arthurian heroes to their creator and his chief spokesman in the book, Doc, the proprietor of Western Biological Laboratory. This character is clearly another literary manifestation of Ed Ricketts, Steinbeck's old friend and mentor. Doc's witty observations add a good deal of humor to the novel, and a few of the "boys' " adventures are really funny. Steinbeck also included a number of completely extraneous stories, many of which amusingly devastate middle-class mores. Much like *Tortilla Flat, Cannery Row* remains a fun book to read, although like the earlier novel it lacks serious subject matter, a realistic style, and true artistic insight. Most of the critics saw it in this light, but the average reader took it to his heart. *Cannery Row* quickly sold to the movies, but for a number of reasons it did not go into production until the 1980s. This 1982 film version will be considered in chronological order below; filmed a generation after it was published, its significance exists in its contemporary view of Steinbeck.

The significance of *Cannery Row* for Steinbeck's literary career was its intention as no more than simple entertainment. Steinbeck wanted to escape the war, and in April 1944 he wrote to a friend: ". . . working every day on a silly book that is fun anyway."[6] The wartime reading public agreed with him and bought his little book avidly.

Though its value as entertainment cannot be faulted, *Cannery Row* was a serious literary comedown for the author of *The Grapes of Wrath*. Its publication indicated his complete inability to absorb the war, the central event of the decade, into his artistic vision. *The Moon Is Down, Bombs Away!, Lifeboat, A Medal for Benny,* and *Cannery Row* chart a course from serious, if unsuccessful engagement to complete disengagement with the war. During the war, the developments in American culture as well as of his own life formed Steinbeck's career in patterns opposite to his course in the 1930s, when he was moving toward documentary commitment and social engagement. Steinbeck's development had faltered during the war years, but 1945 was a definite turning point. With *Cannery Row* he definitively opted for escape, popularity, and success. Undoubtedly he was uneasy over his choices; his biographer reports heavy drinking and marital tensions.[7] Yet once the choice was made, there was no turning back. Steinbeck had lost the artistic vision that had once made him the most important American writer of the 1930s. It could well be said that he had lost it at the movies, as the 1982 film version of *Cannery Row* would attest posthumously.

4

The Postwar Period

I. AFTER THE WAR

John Steinbeck was forty-three when World War II ended in 1945; he died in 1968 at the age of sixty-six. Over those twenty-odd years, Steinbeck was to be extremely productive, winning considerable acclaim—most notably, the Nobel Prize for literature in 1962. Yet the really important part of his career was finished. The war had changed the direction of his artistic development, and Steinbeck seemed powerless to reverse his decline.

He tried again and again to write his way back to the artistic success of his earlier years, notably in *The Wayward Bus* (1947), but his commercial success kept getting in the way. *East of Eden* (1952), Steinbeck's major postwar novel, attempted another California epic to match the grandeur of *The Grapes of Wrath* (1940). Although the book was a blockbuster best seller, it was an artistic and critical failure. Steinbeck himself seemed to recognize his own decline, and in his last years he virtually abandoned fiction for journalism.

Interestingly enough, of all the fiction Steinbeck wrote in his later career, the most artistically successful was occasioned by film projects involving Mexico. His novel *The Pearl* (1947) and his screenplay *Viva Zapata!* (1952) remain his most honest literary works of the postwar period. In order to explain their success, as well as the failure of *East of Eden* and the later works, we must analyze Steinbeck's developing relationship with the technique of film and with the subject matter of Mexico.

As indicated above, Steinbeck's major fiction had responded to the documentary thrust of American film during the Depression decade. His best work was filmic in the best sense of that word—visual, realistic, objective. These qualities nicely balanced the allegorical and romantic strains inherent in his earlier fiction. During World War II his work developed in the direction of movies, not film. In fact, much of his postwar writing seems to find its inspiration in Hollywood versions of his work. His own screen adaptation of an earlier story, *The Red Pony* (1949), is a sentimentalized reproduction of the original. Still he was occasionally capable of recapturing his truly filmic vision, particularly in his works about Mexico—*The Pearl* and *Viva Zapata!*

Mexico always had been an important symbolic place for Steinbeck. As a native Californian, he had been aware of his state's Mexican heritage. Even as a boy he sought out Mexican-American companions, fascinated by their unconcern for the pieties of WASP culture; he also befriended Mexican fieldhands at the ranches where he worked during his college summers.[1] Later his first literary success, *Tortilla Flat*, grew from his involvement with the *paisanos* of Monterey, people who would today be called Chicanos. Appropriately, the money Steinbeck made on the screen rights to *Tortilla Flat* enabled him to take his first trip to Mexico in 1935. He stayed for several months, enjoying his happiest days with his first wife. His next visit was the Sea of Cortez expedition in 1940, a voyage which elicited Steinbeck's most carefully developed scientific and philosophical writing. In the same year Steinbeck visited Mexico twice more in connection with the filming of *The Forgotten Village*, his only screen documentary. It seems natural, therefore, that during the personal and artistic crisis which followed his harsh experiences of war, Steinbeck would return to Mexico, this time with his second wife. Meetings with old friends there ended in the suggestion that he write a screenplay for a Mexican film.[2] Steinbeck agreed, and after a stay of several months he came back to New York to begin the new Mexican work after he finished *Cannery Row.*

Steinbeck's earlier works about the *paisanos,* as well as *The Forgotten Village,* indicate the reason for his fascination with Mexico. Basically that country was everything modern America was not; for him Mexico possessed a primitive vitality, a harsh simplicity, and a romantic beauty—all of which are found in *The Pearl.* Mexico is shown to have the same qualities in the works of other modern writers such as Malcolm Lowery, Aldous Huxley, Graham Greene, Hart Crane, and Katherine Anne Porter. All of them lived and worked there for some time, and the traditional culture they discovered there contrasted sharply with the apparent sterility of the modern world north of the border. Steinbeck was fascinated by a Mexico still alive with social concern. The continued extension of the revolution into the countryside had been his subject in *The Forgotten Village,* and it would be developed further in *Viva Zapata!* For Steinbeck, Mexico came to represent the artistic purity and social purpose he had lost after World War II.

This sense of the writer's personal involvement energizes *The Pearl,* making it Steinbeck's best work of fiction since *The Grapes of Wrath* in 1939. At its beginning the storyteller states: "If this story is a parable, perhaps everyone takes his own meaning from it and reads his own life into it."[3] The critics have read Steinbeck's little parable in a number of ways, but strangely enough they have not considered it as an allegory of the author's own life in the postwar period. Much like Ernest Hemingway's *The Old Man and The Sea* (1952), Steinbeck's *The Pearl* uses the life of a simple fisherman in the symbolic investigation of an aging artist's difficult maturation.

II. THE PEARL

Steinbeck began work on *The Pearl* shortly after he completed *Cannery Row*. He wrote quickly and finished the story, then titled *The Pearl of La Paz*, in early February, 1945. It appeared ten months later in the December issue of *Woman's Home Companion* under the title "The Pearl of the World." Book publication took two more years, because the book was tied to the release of the movie version.[1] In 1945, Steinbeck, Jack Wagner (his coauthor on *A Medal For Benny),* and Mexican movie director Emilio Fernandez rewrote the story as a screenplay. Financial difficulties slowed the production until 1947, when it was backed by RKO which released the film version in the United States early in 1948, the first Mexican-made film to win general release in American theaters.[2] During its long gestation period, the movie wandered a good distance from Steinbeck's original story. Although the film is at best a curiosity, the story which inspired it remains a very fine piece of writing.

Steinbeck was presented with the tale during his Mexican expedition in 1940. In *The Sea of Cortez* he recounts "an event which happened at La Paz in recent years."[3] The story matches the basic outline of *The Pearl*, though Steinbeck makes several major changes, changes significant in an autobiographical sense. In the original, the Mexican fisherman is a devil-may-care bachelor; in *The Pearl* he becomes the sober young husband and father, Kino. Steinbeck himself had just become a father for the first time when he wrote the novelette, and this change provides a clue to the autobiographical nature of the parable. The original bachelor thought the pearl a key to easy living; Kino sees it as a means to create a better way of life for the people through an education for his baby son, Coyotito. If Coyotito could read and write, then he could set his family and his people free from the social and economic bondage in which they toil. Again the allegory suggests the author's life; he believed material success as a writer would bring the opportunity to study, to write, to create. Kino is ignorant of the dangers of wealth, and *The Pearl* is the tale of how he matures by coming to understand them. Steinbeck, too, matured from his youthful innocence as he felt the pressures of success.

As in his best fiction of the 1930s Steinbeck fuses his universal allegory with filmic realism. Perhaps planning ahead for a screenplay, Steinbeck's prose in the novel often takes a cinematic point of view. Scenes are presented in terms of establishing shots, medium views, and close-ups. In particular, Steinbeck carefully examines the natural setting, often visually contrasting human behavior with natural phenomena. As in his best fiction, his naturalistic vision is inherent in the movement of his story, and not an external addition.

Baja California, so scientifically observed on the Sea of Cortez expedition, proves the perfect setting for the realization of his vision. His characters are real people in a real world, but they are also univeral types. Kino, the fisherman named for an early Jesuit explorer, Juana, his wife, and Coyotito, their baby, are almost an archetypal family, like the Holy Family in a medieval morality. Kino's aspirations are the same universal drives to better himself and his family that took the Okies to the California valleys. Like the Joads, this symbolic family must simultaneously struggle against an indifferent natural order and a corrupt social order.

The natural order is represented in the opening description; they live in a harmony with nature represented by the "Song of the Family" which wells up from Kino's soul as he contemplates his wife and child. The harsh side of nature is seen in the incident which initiates the plot; little Coyotito is stung by a scorpion. Nature is not malevolent; the scorpion acts only in self-defense, but his sting may kill the child.

Human corruption threatens the baby when the local doctor refuses to treat him without payment; thus the social concerns of *The Forgotten Village* are reiterated in *The Pearl*.

Kino reacts with indignation, smashing his fist against the
doctor's door which is slammed in his face. Still his anger will
not save his baby; he crushed the scorpion, but he cannot
crush the social order. He resolves to find a pearl to bribe the
greedy doctor.

Steinbeck's description of the pearl beds scientifically
defines his central symbol. As a fact of nature a pearl proves
analogous to the scorpion's sting, a natural process of irrita-
tion and defense.

> The gray oysters with ruffles like skirts on the shells,
> the barnacle-crusted oysters with little bits of weed clinging
> to the skirts and small crabs clinging over them. An acci-
> dent could happen to these oysters, a grain of sand could lie
> in the folds of muscle and irritate the flesh until in self-
> protection the flesh coated the grain with a layer of smooth
> cement. But once started, the flesh continued to coat the
> foreign body until it fell free in some tidal flurry or until the
> oyster was destroyed. For centuries men had dived down
> and torn the oysters from the beds and ripped them open,
> looking for the coated grains of sand. Swarms of fish lived
> near the bed to live near the oysters thrown back by the
> searching men and to nibble at the shining inner shells. But
> the pearls were accidents, and the finding of one was luck, a
> little pat on the back by God or the gods or both. (Viking,
> 1947—pp. 23–24)

When Kino discovers the rich pearl, Steinbeck's description evokes its symbolic significance: ". . . there it lay, the
great pearl, perfect as the moon. It captured the light and
refined it and gave it back in silver incandescence. It was as
large as a sea-gull's egg. It was the greatest pearl in the
world" (30). Steinbeck balances his prose between scientific
documentation and romantic symbolism—the balance which
always resulted in his finest work. His parable is firmly
anchored in physical reality, as this pearl is both the excre-
tion of an oyster and the symbolic "Pearl of Great Price,"
Kino's very soul.[4]

This interpretation supports the autobiographical reading of *The Pearl*. Kino's act of discovery is no random dive, but a journey into the collective soul where he recreates the "Song of the Pearl," sung by his people for countless centuries. Thus his discovery is a creative act, like the writing of the novel itself.

In the great pearl Kino literally sees a better life as in a crystal ball. He and Juana will be married in the church from which they had earlier been turned away for lack of money, much as they had been spurned by the doctor. They will have new clothes, furniture, a rifle—but most importantly Coyotito will have an education. The child will grow to become a leader of the people, able to command the strange language which keeps the Indians in bondage to a corrupt society.

Of course, that social order cannot accept such a vision. Steinbeck describes the inevitable reaction in naturalistic images.

> The news stirred up something infinitely black and evil in the town; the black distillate was like the scorpion, or like hunger in the smell of food, or like loneliness when love is withheld. The poison sacs of the town began to manufacture venom, and the town swelled and puffed with the pressure of it. (p. 35)

As the doctor, the priest, and the others swarm to Kino's hut:

> Out in the estuary a tight woven school of small fishes glittered and broke water to escape a school of great fishes that drove in to eat them. And in the houses the people could hear the swish of the small ones and the bouncing splash of the great ones as the slaughter went on. The dampness arose out of the Gulf and was desposited on bushes and cacti and on little trees in salty drops. And the night mice crept about on the ground and the little night hawks hunted them silently. (p. 47)

Soon thieves are after the pearl, and the pearl buyers, a trust controlled by one rich man, also try to cheat Kino out of his reward. Three times Kino has to fight for his treasure and for his life; in the third fight he kills one of his antagonists with his fishing knife. When his house is burned and his canoe broken, Kino realizes that he must leave the village. Help comes from his sensible older brother, who provides moral support and a machete. Kino hopes to cross the mountains to the capital where he may get a fair price for the pearl. Juana pleads with him to give it up, but he refuses, answering "The pearl has become my soul . . . If I give it up I shall lose my soul" (93).

The flight of the family recalls an earlier story in which a *paisano* boy, Pepe Torres, becomes a man while fleeing the avengers of a drunkard he killed in a brawl. Written in the mid-1930s, "Flight" was published in *The Long Valley* (1938); thus *The Pearl* can be connected directly to the most successful artistic period of Steinbeck's career.

Like Pepe, Kino is reduced to a near animal state by his panic. However, when he is cornered in a mountain cave, he discovers his essential manhood and turns on his pursuers. Just as he coils to spring at them, one fires his rifle into the cave in response to Coyotito's frightened cry. The killer falls under Kino's machete; his henchmen fall to the captured rifle. Kino's child then dies of a human sting more deadly and evil than any scorpion's.

This tragedy resolves Kino's course of action. He and Juana return to the town, she bearing the burden of their dead child, he the captured rifle and the fateful pearl.

> The people say that the two seemed to be removed from human experience; that they had gone through pain and had come out on the other side; that there was almost a magical protection about them. And those people who had rushed to see them crowded back and let them pass and did not speak to them. (p. 120)

They march to the lagoon where he had found the pearl, and then Kino casts it back into the sea, where it settles to the sandy bottom. Thus ends Steinbeck's complex parable of the pearl.

The ambiguity of the final action has led to as many readings of the story as there have been critics. It is seen as an act of regression or retreat, of defiance or despair, of renunciation or reconciliation. In autobiographical terms it seems an act of recognition. Kino lost his soul in finding it; the pearl he found for his son cost him his son. Now he must lose his own soul in order to find it once more. The pearl is "gray and ulcerous" (117) in his hand before he throws it away; in the sea, "the lights on its surface were green and lovely" (118). Kino, matured and hardened, armed with his captured rifle, stands as Steinbeck's Zapata was to stand—a strong but disillusioned hero.

It is not hard to read Steinbeck's postwar disillusionment into Kino's vision. The writer had achieved the success he had dreamed of as a young man, but somehow it kept him from writing what he wanted to create in the first place. Kino's enemies can be seen as the forces with which Steinbeck struggled and to which he lost his youthful innocence. Kino's quest ends in tragedy, but in his tragic struggle and loss, he gains the insight necessary to reject the pearl as the material symbol of the success he should have sought for only in his own soul. Would that his creator, John Steinbeck, could have made the same symbolic gesture of reassertion and put his new vision to work in the creation of mature fictions. Unfortunately, only one later work, the screenplay for *Viva Zapata!*, rises to the level of his novella *The Pearl*. Unlike *The Pearl*, that work fortunately received the film treatment it deserved.

Basically, the anomalous nature of the film version of *The Pearl* may be attributed to its mixed parentage. Conceived as a realistic parable by Steinbeck, the movie became a romantic allegory on the dangers of wealth. It seems doubtful Hollywood would have done much with *The Pearl;* one can imagine the stereotyped characters and the obligatory happy

ending in the manner of *The Red Pony*. The Mexican production avoids these dangers, but is weakened by the self-
conscious artistic aspirations of the moviemakers and the
entertainment anticipations of the audience.

The movie does try to replicate Steinbeck's images with
a sense of artistic purpose. Director Emilio Fernandez,
Mexico's best known *auteur*, and his cinematographer, Gabrial Figuora, who worked with Greg Toland in Hollywood,
seem to have been greatly influenced by Sergei Eisenstein's
artistic documentary *Que Viva Mexico!* As a result *The Pearl* is
often too consciously "arty," opening as a series of stiff
tableaux emphasizing first the physical beauty of the land
and sea, and then of Pedro Armendariz and Maria Elena
Marques as Kino and Juana.[5] These scenes foreshadow other
defects from which the entire picture suffers. Both the sets
and costumes are far from realistic. Like their costumes, the
players generally are too pretty and glossy. Neither of the
leads prove very convincing; they do a lot of wide-eyed
staring and speak in a kind of pidgin English which weakens
Steinbeck's supple dialogue. Although this dialogue works on
the page, on the sound track it takes on a pseudo-biblical
quality that never lets the audience forget it is hearing
"movie Mexican" talk. The music is also overdone, especially
in the chase scenes, often making them a little ridiculous.

After the discovery of the pearl, the parade of well-
wishers turns into a fiesta, complete with dancers so prac-
ticed they perform like "Mexican Rockettes" in one reviewer's phrase. This intrusive sequence is followed by another in
which Kino gets drunk in the local tavern, fights with his
companions, and kisses a bar girl. All of this behavior is
completely out of character for Steinbeck's Kino, or even for
the Kino established in the film. In an insightful article on the
film, Charles Metzer suggests that these interpolations may
have been made in terms of audience expectations—both
American and Mexican. American audiences were virtually
conditioned to some Latin *senoritas* dancing to South of the

Border rhythms in any film set in Mexico, while popular Mexican movies invariably appealed to the *macho* sensibilities of their male viewers with scenes of drinking, brawling, and wenching.[6]

The movie is closer to the book in the sequences which describe Kino's ever increasing tension over the pearl. When he takes it to sell to the pearl brokers, he discovers that they have joined against him to offer a ridiculously low price. When he refuses their unfair offer, attempts are made to steal the pearl. In the course of these attacks Kino is beaten and his family terrorized. Finally, Kino is forced to kill one of his assailants with his fishing knife.

In both book and film versions Kino decides to defy the power structure and flee with his family and the pearl to the capital city, where he can sell for a fair price and live in comfort. Of course, the patron has other plans, and he follows after the little family with a pair of Indian trackers. In both versions, the chase is harrowing, though more realistic in Steinbeck's prose, which again recalls his earlier story, "Flight." In the book, Kino and his family are chased and eventually cornered by three men, whom he outwits and kills in desperate rage. In the film they are pursued by two groups, through mangrove swamps, deserts, plains, and mountains. Like a Hollywood Western, the movie equates more action with more entertainment. The film also presents a genuine villain in the *patron* of the pearl brokers (overplayed by Fernando Wagner) who hounds the family. Surprisingly, the film does not alter the grim symbolism of Steinbeck's ending.

The overall effect is a confusion of purposes—part artistic documentary, part musical, part Western, part allegory. Steinbeck's characters are weakened, his plot unnecessarily complicated if not compromised, his themes simplified. The film completely loses the essential and complex theme of striving and success with all its autobiographical undertones. Instead it becomes an almost Faustian allegory on the corruption of wealth.

After the credits, the film opens with a long shot of the
Baja California coastal ranges. A narrator's voice simplifies
the subtle prose of Steinbeck's introduction as we are treated
to a series of Eisensteinian shots in which stark figures are
posed against the seascape. It is the seventh day of a storm
which has kept the fisherman from the sea. Kino contemplates the cruel sea with all the stolid look of a cigar-store
Indian, and then returns to his hut. The purpose of this
maritime prologue proves puzzling. The sea represents nature, of course, and the storm nature's indifference to human
needs. This sequence and the later views of the fishing boat
seem reminiscent of another "poetic" documentary, Robert
Flaherty's *Man of Aran* (1934); perhaps director Fernandez is
paying homage to another cinematic source.

The scene at Kino's hut stays closer to Steinbeck's text,
but again it is flattened by the set piece compositions and the
unintentionally funny dialogue about tortillas and beans
rendered in "movie Mexican." Steinbeck's simple "Song of
the Family" finds its way onto the sound track, a welcome
relief after the symphonic background to the sea shots. The
scorpion sequence is skillfully handled in a series of deft
close-ups of the baby in his crib. This tight expressionless
style proves the film's best mode, in contrast to the obviously heroic posing of characters against the sky and sea at
the outset.

The expedition to the Doctor's is also well handled, and
Charles Rooner's characterization of the corrupt practitioner
is much in the spirit of Steinbeck's original. Kino's rage at his
rejection leads him back to the angry sea. The launching of
the boats again recalls *Man of Aran*, while the underwater
shots are very beautifully photographed. Pedro Armendariz
seems to be working without a double, and his strong, athletic
body looks capable of the feats Kino performs. The discovery
of the great pearl again deftly manipulates close-ups, capturing some of the mystical beauty of Steinbeck's central symbol, but once again the sequence is undercut by Kino's roar of

victory as he waves his fist against the sky, almost defying the Gods in a Faustian gesture.

On shore, the news of the pearl is spread by means of a neat montage, which ends with the assembly of a *mariachi* band. At this point the work becomes two—one an arty film following Steinbeck's text, the other a popular movie. Musical sequences worthy of MGM's Freed Unit are thrice intercut with Kino's Expressionistic dreams for the future. While these songs and dances may have momentarily entertained the general audience, they make any serious viewing of the pearl as symbol nearly impossible.

The same effect is created by the interpolated action sequences. Kino is swept along by his vision, shouting out that he is "a rich man," again almost a *macho* challenge to the universe. The emphasis on Kino's antagonists changes from the priest and the doctor, to a pair of peddlers who are in reality agents of the vicious *patron*. They take Kino out on the town, get him drunk, and provide him with a prostitute. The bar and brothel scenes are not so much bad in themselves as contrary to Steinbeck's characterization of Kino.

During his night of debauchery, it is Juana who protects the pearl, hiding it from the *patron*'s agents. The next day Kino again takes charge, marching through the town to the tune of the *mariachi* band with his treasure. The *patron* is the chief pearl buyer, and he obviously lusts after this great prize. His attempt at cheating Kino is another well directed scene, with a fine rhythm of close-ups registering the tension of the confrontation. Another focusing device is the use of the pearl buyer's magnifying glass, introduced to dupe Kino into believing his pearl is flawed. Of course, the pearl looks porous in magnification, and Kino is puzzled until Juana holds the glass up to his eye creating a similar effect. The glass reinforces the theme of deceptive appearances, later to be demonstrated in the *patron*'s treachery.

Kino is not deceived by the *patron*'s tricks, however, and he resolves to take his pearl to another city for a better price.

As in the novel, Juana asks him to give it up, but he answers that the pearl has become his freedom. When Juana tries to throw the pearl back into the sea, Kino knocks her to the ground. Again the movie raises the ante of violent action when the *patron's* two agents attack Kino with drawn knives. Their death struggle in the roaring surf is pretty exciting action, though it again reduces Steinbeck's story to a thriller.

When Kino and his family decide to flee, their boat is swamped by the same raging surf, forcing them to make their way on foot through the mangrove swamps. They are pursued by the doctor with a savage tracking dog, as well as by the *patron* with two Indian trackers. The *patron* quickly dispatches his rival, allowing the family to escape in the confusion. The swamp sequence is well photographed, but the subsequent chase at night across the arid plains is obviously shot in daylight with a dark filter, creating the visual effect of a low budget Western. This chase is punctuated by another killing, that of the old *soltero*, or hermit, who provides the fleeing family with food and water. The confrontation in the "mountains" (rather like scaled down versions of John Ford's Monument Rocks) follows Steinbeck rather closely. Again symbolic close-ups of the pearl and the baby are well done, but the use of dark filters and the almost ludicrous poses of the *patron* and Kino against the sky undercut the drama of the showdown.

The final sequence, the return to the village, is perhaps the only one to capture the full power of Steinbeck's original vision. The narrator returns to draw a rather obvious moral from the story, but the visuals elevate his comments. Armandariz and Marques fully project the real Kino and Juana for the first time as they trudge through the streets toward the sea. No *mariachi* bands play, nor do any false heroics intrude. After he casts the pearl back into the raging sea, the camera closes up on their clasped hands, and the final title is placed next to their stark figures outlined against a setting sun.

If the entire film was of the quality of the final sequence,

The Pearl might have been a notable work of art, comparable to Steinbeck's short novel. The director's cinematic pretensions and the producer's commercial compromises confused its purposes, converting the movie into little more than a curiosity of Mexican studio production. Any lasting importance it might have exists in terms of its connections to the short novel by John Steinbeck which served as its source, and which like his screenplay *Viva Zapata!* was one of his most significant postwar creations.

III. THE RED PONY

While Steinbeck was in Mexico conferring on the screenplay of *The Pearl* in April of 1945 another film project was proposed to him—a screen biography of Mexican revolutionary hero Emiliano Zapata.[1] Aware of the Zapata legend since his first Mexican journey, he was immediately interested by the project. Many delays ensued, and Steinbeck's vision of Zapata was not to appear on the screen for another seven years.

It was during the same Mexican visit in 1945 that Steinbeck also conceived his next novel, the story of a busload of Mexican peasants and American tourists making a difficult pilgrimage across the sierra. When he returned home to work on the book, Steinbeck changed its setting to California and gave it a title, *The Wayward Bus*. He probably decided to write the novel before the Zapata screenplay because he had begun to blame his literary decline on his diversion into the movies.[2]

Steinbeck intended *The Wayward Bus* to be a big book, his most important since *The Grapes of Wrath*. Like the earlier novel it utilized the journey motif, and it centered on a symbolic vehicle much like that in *Lifeboat*. Steinbeck found the writing of it difficult, perhaps because his energy was being drained by domestic strife. After the birth of his second son, his second marriage went to pieces.[3] As a result, a good deal of his resentment of American marital life found its way into *The Wayward Bus,* which proved a rambling failure. Steinbeck himself seemed aware of its problems; at one point he decided to shelve the project, but was talked out of this move by his publisher.[4] Once again commercial expediency took precedence over literary development. When the novel appeared in 1947 it was generally well received by the public, but the critics were much harsher in their judgments. A best seller, the novel was quickly sold to the movies, but for a number of reasons it did not become a film until 1957.

Later in 1947, Steinbeck made a literary journey to the Soviet Union in the company of photographer Robert Capa. The result of their observations was the documentary book *A Russian Journal* (1948), which strikingly demonstrated Steinbeck's real talent for objective, yet sensitive journalism. At a time when the Cold War was beginning to freeze the relationship between the Eastern and Western power blocs, he provided a basically sympathetic portrait of a people whose lives were seriously constricted by the totalitarian government under which they lived. Capa's fine photographs seem to have inspired Steinbeck's prose to a corresponding level of craft. Once again a realistic, documentary framework was to result in one of his best writing efforts. The book was well reviewed and Steinbeck gained a reputation as something of an expert on public affairs.

Following the publication of *A Russian Journal* and *The Pearl* in 1948, Steinbeck began work on a major project. Originally called *Salinas Valley,* this big novel about California was meant to restore his declining reputation for literary fiction. Four years later it was finished as *East of Eden.* Work on his intended masterpiece was slowed by a number of personal problems. To the tension of a second divorce was added the grief occasioned by the accidental death of Ed Ricketts in 1948. In addition, during this same period Steinbeck turned out another short play-novel, *Burning Bright* (1950), a new version of *The Log From the Sea of Cortez* (1951), and two film projects: *The Red Pony* (1949) and *Viva Zapata!* (1952).

The Red Pony was a labor of love both for the writer and Lewis Milestone, who in 1939 had directed the sensitive screen version of *Of Mice and Men*. Having become friendly during the production of the earlier film, the pair had discussed the possibility of bringing *The Red Pony* to the screen as early as 1940.[5] However, various other projects kept both men from working on the scheme until 1947 when they went into partnership to make the film version. A number of problems delayed both the production and its release until 1949. Steinbeck served as screenwriter, his only solo adaptation of one of his own works, while Milestone took on the jobs of both producer and director.

Unfortunately, though aided by a capable production team and cast, Steinbeck and Milestone turned out only a competent screen version which proved a moderate success, both critically and financially. The artistic climate of the Hollywood studio system prevented a fully realized film version of *The Red Pony*. *Of Mice and Men*, though an artistic success, did not fit box-office formula and so had failed commercially even when in desperation the Roach studios had tried to peddle it as a sex shocker. If similar financial failure were to be avoided, *The Red Pony* had to be refashioned and pigeonholed as a kind of kiddy Western about a boy and his horse. The film's conclusion, altered to a stock happy ending, is representative of the general transformation of plot, character, and theme in this cinematic adaptation of one of Steinbeck's finest works of fiction.

Steinbeck evidently began *The Red Pony* fairly early in his career; his letters indicate he was working on a "pony story" in 1933, and the first two sections of the story sequence, "The Gift" and "The Great Mountains" were published in the *North American Review* for November and December of that year. The third section, "The Promise" did not appear in *Harpers* until 1937, and "The Leader of the People", the final section, was not added until the publication of *The Long Valley* in 1938. However, manuscript and textual evidence indicates that the later sections were written some time before their publication, not very long after the first two stories.[6] The four sections are connected by common characters, settings, and themes, forming a clearly unified story sequence which was published separately as *The Red Pony* in 1945.

All four stories involve the maturation of Jody Tiflin, a boy of about ten when the action opens. The time is about 1910 and the setting is the Tiflin ranch in the Salinas Valley, where Jody lives with his father, Carl, his mother, Ruth, and the hired hand, a middle-aged cowboy named Billy Buck. From time to time they are visited by Jody's grandfather, a venerable old man who led one of the first wagon trains to California. "The Gift," the first story in the sequence, concerns Jody's red pony, which he names Gabilan, after the nearby mountain range. The pony soon becomes a symbol of the boy's growing maturity and his developing knowledge of the natural world. Later he carelessly leaves the pony out in the rain, and it takes cold and dies, despite Billy Buck's efforts to save it. Thus Jody learns of nature's cruel indifference to human wishes. In the second section, "The Great Mountains," the Tiflin ranch is visited by a former resident, Gitano, an aged Chicano laborer raised in the now vanished *hacienda*. Old Gitano had come home to die. In a debate which recalls Robert Frost's poem "The Death of the Hired Man," Carl persuades Ruth that they cannot take Old Gitano in, but as in the poem their dialogue proves pointless. Stealing a broken-down nag significantly named Easter, the old man rides off into the mountains to die in dignity. Again, Jody has discovered some of the complex, harsh reality of adult life.

In "The Promise," the third story, Jody learns of the inextricable connections between life and death, when to get the boy another colt, his father has one of the mares put to stud. However, the birth is complicated, and Billy Buck must kill the mare to save the colt. "The Leader of the People," brings the sequence to an end with another vision of death and change. Jody's grandfather comes to visit, retelling his timeworn stories of the great wagon crossing. Carl Tiflin cruelly hurts the old man by revealing that nobody but Jody is really interested in these repetitious tales. The grandfather realizes that Carl is right, but later he tells Jody that the adventurous stories weren't the point, but that his message was "Westering" itself. For the grandfather, "Westering" was a force like Turner's frontier, the source of American identity; now with the close of the frontier, "Westering" has ended. Westerners had degenerated to petty landholders like Carl Tiflin and aging cowboys like Billy Buck. In his grandfather's ramblings, Jody discovers a sense of mature purpose, and by the conclusion of the sequence he too can hope to be a leader of the people.

This story sequence is among Steinbeck's finest work. *The Red Pony* traces Jody's initiation into adult life with both realism and sensitivity, a balance which Steinbeck did not always achieve. The vision of the characters caught up in the harsh world of nature is balanced by their deep human concerns and commitments. The evocation of the ranch setting in its vital beauty is matched only in the author's finest works, such as *Of Mice and Men*. Steinbeck's symbols grow naturally out of this setting, and nothing in the story sequence seems forced into a symbolic pattern, as is true in the later works. In its depiction of an American variation of a universal experience, *The Red Pony* deserves comparison with the finest of American fiction, especially initiation tales such as Faulkner's *The Bear* or Hemingway's Nick Adams stories.

Obviously, such a fine work of fiction had much to offer as a film, but it also represented some inherent difficulties. Steinbeck's story sequence is episodic, unified only by continuities of character, setting, and theme. These subtle variations on the theme of intiation had to be woven together and considerably cut for a screenplay. The exigencies of production forced Steinbeck to eliminate completely one of the four stories in the sequence, "The Great Mountains," and to severely cut another one, "The Promise." For adaptation purposes the remaining stories were then spliced to form a sequential narrative of considerably less complexity. In addition Steinbeck concluded his screenplay with a Hollywood happy ending that completely distorts the meaning of his original work.

Though characters, particularly Jody and his grandfather, are types, they are complex ones and therefore hard to realize. Of the cast only Robert Mitchum as the ranchhand Billy Buck remains convincing throughout the movie, and even Mitchum is too youthful and idealized. In many ways he seems a variation of another idealized screen character created by Alan Ladd a few years later in *Shane* (1953). As in George Stevens's film, though not in Steinbeck's story, the relationship between the ranch wife and the hired hand becomes a complicating issue in Milestone's movie. Myrna Loy and Mitchum, who were given the star billing for the film, create a sense of romance between the characters they portray. Perhaps trying to escape her role as William Powell's sophisticated spouse in the Thin Man series, Miss Loy strains to be sweet in her role as Alice Tiflin. (For some reason, Steinbeck changed the name of all three Tiflins from novel to screenplay.)[7] Fred Tiflin is weaker and less interesting than in the story sequence, and he is made even less so by Shepperd Strudwick's hangdog interpretation. Louis Calhern is adequate though uninspired as the grandfather. However the major casting problem is with the protagonist, Tom Tiflin, as portrayed by Peter Miles. Perhaps no child star could capture the complexity of this role, as it is much easier to write about sensitive children than to film them. Young Miles's portrayal often seems rather sugared and his anger at the world more or less a tantrum.[8] The only other characters of note are a group of Tom's schoolmates, whose Our Gang antics make Peter Miles's performance seem peerless by comparison.

The other production values are good. The film was shot on location at a Salinas Valley ranch that looks very much like the one used in *Of Mice and Men*. As in the earlier film, settings are very well handled with realistic interiors and natural exteriors. Tony Gaudio's color cinematography makes use of natural, muted tones which often suggest the best of regional American painting and sometimes Wesley Dennis's illustrations for the 1945 edition of *The Red Pony*. Perhaps the best single feature of the film is the powerful score by Aaron Copeland, who had also scored *Of Mice and Men;* both scores later became concert favorites. As in his earlier work for Milestone, Copeland matches the mood of the visuals.

Milestone opens the film with a pre-title sequence which clearly recalls *Of Mice and Men* in both visual and musical imagery. As in the earlier film, the sequence establishes a complex relationship between the human characters and the natural world. First the camera pans over a scenic spot of the dark mountains, at last establishing the ranch house and outbuildings nestled in a hollow. A narrative voice-over establishes time and place:

> In central California many small ranches sit in the hollows of the skirts of the Coast Range Mountains. Some, the remnants of old and gradually disintegrating homesteads; some the remains of Spanish grants. To one of them in the foothills to the west of Salinas Valley, the dawn comes, as it comes to a thousand others.[9]

The natural cycle of day begins earlier for the animal than the human world. In quick sequence Milestone close-ups a crowing rooster on a post, a gobbling turkey in a tree, two dogs shaking slowly from sleep, a softly hooting owl in another tree, and finally a rabbit. The dogs and the owl respond to the presence of the rabbit just beyond camera range; then the owl swoops for a kill. The natural world presents a complex beauty, marked by rhythms of life and death, of beginnings and endings, of ever repeated cycles. This sequence ends when Billy Buck walks out of the bunk-house and into the barn, lighting a lantern to check the

horses. The light falls on the cover of the novel, which in turn
opens to present the production data—a common title device
in the 1940s. All in all like many Milestone films, *The Red
Pony* opens quite well, but, unfortunately, it does not sustain
the artistic intensity of the beginning.

After the titles fade, Billy whistles and calls his mare,
Rosie; then Billy fondles her and begins a morning ritual of
feeding and currying. Milestone cuts to the farmhouse where
Alice Tiflin is preparing breakfast; she stops and walks out on
the porch to ring the triangle that calls the rest of the
characters. Two quick close-ups show the awakening Fred
Tiflin and his son, Tommy. Billy arrives at the kitchen first,
but he waits for the others to enter before him, subtly
establishing the relationship of the owner and hired hand, as
well as the equation of Tommy and Fred as the immature
members of the family and of Alice and Billy as those who
accept adult responsibility.

Inside the kitchen some homey bits are done: close-ups of
cooking ham and eggs, the boy washing behind the ears, and
the father kidding Billy about a trip into town. At this point
the screenplay includes a long conversation—not included in
the final print—about Billy's mare, Rosie, who is expecting a
colt in a few months. Probably Milestone felt the discussion
slowed the development of the story, even though it
foreshadowed the symbolic birth of Rosie's colt at the conclusion. However, the film does add scenes to the story at this
point. After Billy and Tom leave, Alice and Fred Tiflin's
exchange about Tom's attachment for the ranch hand clearly
indicates the father's sense of inadequacy and his jealousy of
his hired hand. The reason for his anxiety is revealed in the
next sequence, in which Tom asks Billy to show him the
newspaper clipping reporting Rosie's victory in the Sac-
ramento Stock Show. As the best hand with horses in the
area, Billy is nature's nobleman for young Tom, an extension
of his grandfather's days of glory in the Old West.

Milestone dramatizes these feelings, as Tom sets off for

school, fantasizing that he and Billy are knights leading a troop of splendid soldiers. This interpolated sequence includes an animated background which seems right out of a Walt Disney production. Of course, it is intended to visualize the boy's fantasy life, but it only establishes a kids' picture undertone which would have been best avoided here. This mood is underlined by the next scene when Tom's reverie is disturbed by the other school children. In his story, Steinbeck handles both of these sequences in a single sentence: "At the crossroads over the bridge he met two friends and the three of them walked to school together, making ridiculous strides and being rather silly." When this sentence is translated into a combination of Disney and Our Gang, the film quickly loses much of the power promised by the literary source and anticipated in the strong opening sequence.

Meanwhile, back at the ranch, Alice and Fred talk about the expected arrival of the grandfather, and we are introduced to themes from "The Leader of the People." In the film the grandfather owns the ranch and lives with the Tiflin family, and this establishes a relationship which is very different from the one in the story. Fred is made a childish dependent, much like his son, Tom. In this conversation it becomes apparent that he doesn't much like the ranch and longs to return to town life in San Jose. Alice is more thoroughly identified with her father as a symbol of a natural tradition also represented by Billy Buck. When Tom returns from school in the next sequence Alice remembers Fred's complaint that the boy neglects his school work to knock about with Billy. She even repeats her husband's very words. "There are other things to know besides ranching." Her heart is not in her scolding, and she soon allows Tom to leave his books and go off to prowl the ranch yard. Here he feeds the chickens and performs other chores in Tom Sawyer or Huck Finn fashion while Milestone makes a nice overhead shot of the boy circled by the clucking hens. However, animation changes the fowl to white circus horses prancing around a ring while Tom directs them with a long ringmaster's whip. The screenplay indicates that both of these animated fantasy sequences were to have been longer, but Milestone wisely cut them down; he would have been even wiser to cut them out completely.

This time Tom is pulled from his reverie by the call of his arriving grandfather. This scene and the dinner that follows are taken almost verbatim from "The Leader of the People" and intertwined with the themes of "The Gift." Although this process creates some dislocations, it does make the grandfather's story seem less of a digression from the process of Tom's maturation. When Tom tells the grandfather that he plans a mouse hunt after the haystacks are leveled, the grandfather compares the hunt to the cavalry's slaughter of the Indians on the frontier, and Tom learns that the Western experience was not all the imaginings of dime novels. His initiation into the complex realities of adult life continues at dinner when his father slights his grandfather at every opportunity, clearly demonstrating the immaturity hinted at in earlier scenes.

After dinner, the red pony is presented. Billy and Fred bought the animal in town, where it was left stranded by the collapse of a traveling show. Tom, of course, is ecstatic, both with his pony and its show saddle. He promises to take the best possible care of the animal, and to perform all of his other chores faithfully in repayment for the gift. Fred soon leaves, with a final threat to sell the pony if he ever finds it hungry or dirty, and Billy Buck takes over as the father surrogate, promising to help Tom raise the best horse in the region. The pony will be trained well enough to ride by Thanksgiving, Billy assures the boy. Clearly, Gabilan, the red pony, represents a link with primal nature within the natural process of a boy's maturation.

Meanwhile, the child in Tom is revealed when the next day he brings his school friends home to see the pony. Once again the film falls to the level of *My Friend Flicka* (1943), as the kids cut some cute capers only briefly mentioned in

Steinbeck's original work. Better scenes are created when Milestone shows Billy and Tom working with the animal. In many of these ranch scenes the director achieves the naturalistic poetry he created from California ranch life in *Of Mice and Men*. When Tom trains the horse with a rope and halter, the camera pans for 180 degrees on the resulting circle of movement and then rises for a down shot, a composition which clearly reduplicates Wesley Dennis's frontpiece for the illustrated edition of the stories.

The following two sequences combine the climactic action of both "The Leader of the People" and "The Gift." At breakfast, after Tom has shown how well he has trained his horse, his father reacts by bullying both the boy and the grandfather. Thinking that the old man is out of earshot Fred complains bitterly about the grandfather's garrulous tales of his days as wagonmaster. However, the old man overhears him from behind the doorway, and this knowledge embarrasses the whole group gathered for breakfast. Milestone handles this scene very nicely in terms of quick close-up reaction shots that capture it's inherent drama. Fred apologizes and prepares to retreat to his parents' home in San Jose, a clear desertion of his responsibilities to his family and the ranch. The grandfather who must reassess his relationships and his attitudes, concludes that he has indeed bored everyone with his tales. Yet he insists that his purpose was right, he wanted not to tell of wild adventures, but to capture the essence of the Westward movement in his talk. He muses:

> . . . We carried life our here and set it down and planted it the way ants carry eggs and I was the leader. The westerin' was big as God and the slow steps that made up the movement piled up . . . and piled up until the continent was crossed . . . Then we come down to the sea and it was done . . . Well, that's what I oughtta be tellin' instead a' the stories. The Stories ain't what I want to say.[10]

Tom intuitively understands what his grandfather means, and his sympathy for the old man is another indication of his developing maturity. Yet he is not ready to be a leader of the people himself. The experience of loss and death await him.

Partially because of his own carelessness, partially because of Billy Buck's, his beloved pony is left in the corral through a cold and rainy afternoon. When Tom returns from school—a Disney-like scene with byplay between the kids and the teacher played by Margaret Hamilton, the Wicked Witch of the West from *The Wizard of Oz* (1939)—the pony is shivering and sneezing. Tom guiltily accuses Billy Buck of having failed in his responsibility. "You said it wouldn't rain," he whines in protest. The boy has learned another lesson: the adults in his world are fallible. As the pony sickens, he learns more of nature's indifference to human wishes. He may fantasize all he wants about his "trick pony," but nature plays the final trick. Billy cannot save the weakening animal in spite of a promise to pull the pony through. Finally Billy opens a hole in the animal's windpipe in a futile, last attempt to save its life. In a discreet reaction shot, Milestone captures the boy's sensitive response to blood and pain. Naturally, this scene is more powerfully depicted in the story than in a film which had to avoid shocking the sensibilities of it's intended juvenile audience. Even so, some contemporary reviews complained that both this scene and that of the pony's death were too harsh for children.

A couple of sentimental scenes intrude before the pony's death and Tom's fight with buzzards. The mother recalls the father from San Jose, and he pledges his love for her, the boy, and the ranch. On Thanksgiving, when Tom's friends come expecting to see him and ride the pony for the first time, he is forced to put them off with a story about the pony being shod in town. His pride won't allow him to share the hurt he feels for his dying pony. Later that same evening, Tom beds down in the pony's stall, but the animal wanders from the barn, seeking the hills to die in nature. Waking from his fitful sleep, the boy follows the pony's footprints up into the scrubby brush, and looking up, Tom and the camera see a circle of buzzards. Tom runs along the crest of a bare hill as the camera follows him in a long tracking shot. Then in a down angle it catches his running reflection in the pool of a stream; suddenly he stops and reverses direction. The camera looks at the dead pony through Tom's eyes. A buzzard has come down on the body, and as Tom watches another lands near the head. The boy races back down the bank, chasing the buzzards; then the camera follows him past the pony as he grabs a thrusting bird. The camera cuts quickly between the boy and the buzzard, as the frantic bird pecks at him wildly. The bird's beak and claws cut Tom in several places, and as blood soaks his ripped shirt he finds a sharp stone and smashes the buzzard with it. Billy and Fred come running in just as the boy strangles the bird in one final burst of rage. In a line of dialogue taken from the story, Fred tells Tom that the buzzard hasn't killed his pony; and Billy, more perceptive in this crisis, snaps: "Of course he knows it. Use your head, man, can't you see how he'd feel about it?"

It is Billy, not Fred, who carries Tom back to the ranch house. As they retrace the muddy tracks left by the dying pony, Billy expiates his own guilt in the pony's death and the boy's disillusionment by promising to give him Rosie's colt when it is born. This development is taken from the third story in Steinbeck's sequence, "The Promise," in which the events take place about a year after the red pony's death. Here the action is shortened as Billy's mare is nearing the end of her gestation cycle. At first Tom refuses to take any interest in Billy's promise. He has been too badly hurt by the loss of the red pony to chance his feelings on another horse. Instead he rejects Billy, his family and his friends at school. In one fine scene he sits reading and is shown reflected by the stream seen earlier in the death of the pony; Rosie coming to drink nuzzles him gently, but he rejects her as well.

Yet as Spring opens out, the sense of life overpowers the memory of death. Tom again talks to his family and his friends; he begins to play with his dogs and Rosie; finally, he asks Billy for the colt. Billy promises that the mare will drop a fine colt with no complications. But again nature ignores human desires. In a scene recalling the earlier unsuccessful operation on the red pony, Billy encounters unexpected problems with the birth of Rosie's colt. Evidently, it is turned the wrong way in the mother's womb, and the horseman must choose between killing the mother or the colt. In the story the boy watches in horror as Billy brutally fulfills his promise by killing poor Rosie in the process of delivering a beautiful colt. The screenplay, probably under studio pressure, opts for an easier conclusion.

Billy makes the decision to kill Rosie, but Tom grabs the knife and runs off to the house. By the time the ranchhand has caught up with him, the rest of the family are able to prevail on Billy to spare the mother animal. The central group is seen through the doors of Tom's room, then of the house, then of the barn, as they race back to the birth scene. Suddenly, they all stop in amazement as the camera pans them in a row along the side of the stall. Next a point-of-view shot reveals the surprise; somehow in a few moments she was left alone, Rosie has discreetly brought a perfect colt into the world. The pan of the characters is repeated as they all laugh in happy reaction to the bounty of nature. The film's final shots are of Tom riding the mature colt—which bears a decided resemblance to the original red pony—across the beautiful foothills of the Gabilan Mountains.

Of course, this conclusion alters the theme of Steinbeck's story sequence. The author himself included it in his screenplay, perhaps because he felt this final comprise was justified by the realistic presentation of the earlier death of the red pony. Yet this last alteration only typifies the general changes in mood which studio production wrought in the film version of the story sequence. Steinbeck's naturalistic yet beautiful Salinas Valley is transformed into the pastoral dreamland of National Velvet (1944) or The Yearling (1947), or So Dear to My Heart (1949). Some of the characters, particu-

larly Mitchum's Billy Buck, some of the scenes, particularly
the death of the red pony, some of the settings, particularly
the barn, and some of the themes are still reminiscent of
Steinbeck's. In its best places the film adds Milestone's
graceful visual touch and Copland's powerful musical score
to the author's naturalistic, yet lyrical vision.

Although Milestone's *The Red Pony* is not as fully realized
as Steinbeck's original story sequence, it remains a reasonable film adaptation, one much better than most in its generic
pattern. Nevertheless, Steinbeck's complicity in its artistic
compromise indicates how much his ideals had been altered
by Hollywood. There were no telegrams to protest the alteration of his work or asking to remove his name. Perhaps he
needed the money because of his divorce; perhaps he wanted
to see his name on the silver screen once more. In any case,
Steinbeck and Milestone, had both declined as artists since
their happier collaboration on *Of Mice and Men* in 1939.[11]

IV. VIVA ZAPATA!

Only the completely unsuccessful play-novel, *Burning Bright*
(1950) and the revised *Log From the Sea of Cortez* (1951)
separate the screenplays for *The Red Pony* and *Viva Zapata!*
(1952). Steinbeck attempted to rethink his nonteleological
philosophy in *Burning Bright*, a work apparently generated by
his doubts about his writing and his new found personal
optimism. His marriage to Elaine Scott (the former wife of
actor Zachery Scott) provided Steinbeck with a supportive
relationship, but not with adaptable materials. The novel-
play uses three settings (a circus, a farm, and a ship) to relate
its characters in a universal mode, but Steinbeck's language
never matches his ambitious conception. *Burning Bright* remains the most notable instance of the writer's allegorical
penchant gone awry. It received almost entirely negative
reviews, and incited Steinbeck to publish an hysterical re-

joinder to his critics in the pages of *Saturday Review*. The author's counterattack clearly demonstrates his continuing lack of literary confidence, a growing sense that he was developing in the wrong directions. (One notable aspect of his third marriage was his permanent move to New York in 1949.)

During these years Steinbeck worked on both his screen biography of the Mexican revolutionary and his "big" California novel, *East of Eden*, both of which appeared in 1952. Ironically, Steinbeck confused the importance of the two works. He thought *East of Eden* was his *magnum opus* and *Viva Zapata!* just an interesting screenplay. Time has reversed his critical view; *East of Eden* is now generally judged a monumental artistic failure, the final proof of Steinbeck's declining talents, while *Viva Zapata!* has, like his short novel *The Pearl*, come to be appreciated as another honest attempt to recapture his artistic vision. *Viva Zapata!* shares with *The Pearl* a Mexican setting, a careful balance of allegory and realism, and an intense personal identification on the part of the author.

Steinbeck had been interested in Zapata since his first visits to Mexico, and in 1945 he readily agreed to write the screenplay for a Mexican production about the life and times of the revolutionary leader, though he was wary of government interference as Zapata was still a controversial figure in Mexico.[1] Steinbeck delayed the work to write *The Wayward Bus* and the screenplay for *The Red Pony;* further setbacks were caused by financial difficulties on the part of the Mexican production company. Steinbeck visited Mexico to check on the project in 1948, and when it appeared unlikely that the film would ever be made as planned, he mentioned the project to a New York friend, theatrical and film director Elia Kazan. Kazan was at the height of his career after the success of his stage versions of Arthur Miller's and Tennessee Williams's plays, and of several socially realistic films for 20th Century-Fox producer Darryl Zanuck. Kazan could di-

rect what he wanted in Hollywood, and when Steinbeck
interested him in the Zapata biography, the director soon
sold Zanuck on the idea.[2]

Steinbeck finished the screenplay in 1949 and passed it
on to Kazan for editing and revision.[3] A final version was
polished in 1950 after a visit to Mexico with Kazan to scout
locations.[4] As Steinbeck had anticipated, there was indeed
interference from the Mexican government and the production became entirely American. Most of the film was shot on
location along the Texas side of the Rio Grande in the Spring
of 1951. The movie was released early in 1952 to mixed
reviews and an indifferent public response. Since Zanuck
never had much faith in the project, the studio withdrew
publicity support, limiting the film's distribution and popular impact.[5] Over the years, it has become something of a cult
film, popular with television late-show viewers, college film
classes, and Chicano groups.

Viva Zapata! was a controversial film from its inception,
and it remains so to the present. Its controversy is inherent in
both its subject and style. The film promises to be a realistic
biography, almost a documentary; however, Emiliano Zapata
was a colorful, contradictory, somewhat mysterious figure,
obscured by the mists of history and legend. Although his role
in the Mexican revolution remains ambiguous, after his death
in 1919 he became a symbolic figure, a symbol of the incor-
ruptible rebel. Certainly, Zapata was a passionate revolutionary, a charismatic leader dedicated to the cause of land
reform, but he also exhibited many less inspiring traits—
cruelty, greed, and personal vanity.[6] It seems obvious that
Steinbeck's Zapata is an idealized figure. This characterization runs counter to the film's commitment to realistic
biography, and it drew the fire of many critics. In the
politically sensitive atmosphere of the early 1950s, Steinbeck's portrait of Zapata roused critical anger from both
Right and Left. The Right claimed the real Zapata was little
more than a bloodthirsty bandit, while the Left objected to

Zapata's idealistic rejection of power. After 1952 both Steinbeck and Kazan, the only director of stature to cooperate in
the HUAC Hollywood probe, were accused of being disillusioned Liberals, "Cold Warriors" who used the figure of
Zapata to belittle legitimate revolutionary aspirations.[7] According to left-wing critics *Viva Zapata!* emphasizes the
impossibility of any meaningful revolution.

When the film is viewed against the background of
Steinbeck's literary development these charges seem spuri-
ous. Obviously, Zapata is a symbolic figure, "a leader of the
people," in the manner of Tom Joad. Like young Joad, Zapata
is slow to social action, much less rebellion. Like all of
Steinbeck's leaders, the people pick him to save them. The
oppressive absentee landlords of *Viva Zapata!* inevitably recall the large landowners in California's agricultural valleys.
Far from denying the possibility of revolution, Zapata's
reluctance to seize power indicates Steinbeck's belief—
already demonstrated in *The Grapes of Wrath*—that revolution is a natural rather than a political process; in other
words, the essential needs of the people provide a stimulus to
leadership on the part of the "natural" leader. The film
clearly asserts the legitimacy of armed revolution in Zapata's
speech to Madero, during which the hero uses his own rifle to
symbolize the power which proceeds from a gun barrel. The
transformation of the revolutionary army into agarian re-
formers is carefully presented in the film; Zapata's people are
not the vulgar stereotypes of Mexican bandits in the typical
Hollywood movie. Finally, the film condemns weak idealists
like Madero, who lack the practical power to make the
revolution work.

Steinbeck's Zapata does renounce power, but he does so
only when he feels that the goals of the people's revolution
have been achieved. As he tells his wife shortly before his
death: "A strong man makes a weak people. Strong people
don't need a strong man"(114).[8] More importantly, Zapata
recognizes in the exercise of power the temptation of excess.

When he temporarily becomes President, he is transformed into the mold of all the tyrants who have preceded him in the office, particularly into the person of Diaz, the ruthless dictator overthrown by the original revolutionary thrust. Zapata does not reject'the revolution or its goals, rather he renounces the corruptions of power and success in order to save his own soul. In this act he returns to the people, and though treacherously killed by his successors in power, he remains with his people in spirit. Steinbeck's Zapata begins as Tom Joad and like him he is transformed into Jim Casy, a Christ figure who will die for the good of the people. Like Kino in *The Pearl,* Zapata casts away the glittering symbol of success in order to find his true strength in his own soul, which—as Casy did—he recognizes as the soul of his people. In the final analysis Zapata is another of Steinbeck's autobiographical heroes, another surrogate of the author himself, struggling to find his role in life.

Unlike the more allegorical work, *The Pearl, Viva Zapata!* presents this central figure with great complexity and realism. Steinbeck creates a number of figures to dramatize Zapata's psychological complexity. The most obvious of them is Fernando Aguirre, an intellectual and writer who attaches himself to Zapata as a sort of unofficial advisor. Fernando is a cold, relentless, inhuman idealogue, dedicated to his singleminded vision. When Zapata leaves the Presidency, Fernando refuses to go with him, and, as Zapata predicts, he soon is working for Zapata's enemies. In political terms, Fernando is the symbol of Stalinism, and he stands for the political subordination of means to ends. In autobiographical terms, Fernando is obviously the intellectual writer who sells out for worldly power and wealth. In at least one sense, he is what Steinbeck himself had become, just as the film's Zapata is what Steinbeck might have been—the leader who remained true to himself in spite of the blandishments of success.

Although the other characters are not so readily identifiable with Steinbeck, they provide cross-references for judging

Zapata on both a personal and political plane. The characters closest to Zapata personally are largely Steinbeck's creations, based on shadowy historical figures; in contrast, the political personalities are well known and well documented. For example, Fernando was not an historical figure, but he was equated with the historical person of General Huerta. Zapata's other advisors are his brother, Eufemio, and his old friend, Pablo. Like Fernando, Pablo has no historical model, in fact he seems created to contrast with the soulless intellectual. Pablo is like Zapata, a man of the people; in his dealings with them he is warm, sympathetic, and trusting. He is closely tied to the historical Francisco Madero, the weak liberal who ruled as the first revolutionary president. Both men are sensitive to a fault, a condition that paralyzes them when they are confronted with the hard realities of their revolutionary world.

Eufemio, by contrast, has been hardened by conflict and betrayal until he cynically exploits the revolution for his own gain. In the film, he is connected with Pancho Villa, who in turn is presented with some of the Wallace Beery stereotyping that Hollywood grafted onto the historical reality of Mexico's other popular revolutionary hero. Eufemio is based on Zapata's real brother, just as Josefa is based on Zapata's real wife. Both characters were rather obscure historical figures, however. In fact, historians were unaware of Josefa until Steinbeck rediscovered her in his research on Zapata's private life.[9] The real Zapata was reputed to have fathered a sizable brood of bastards,[10] but Steinbeck creates a tender romance with a middle-class girl, and he only hints at *macho* infidelities. Of course, this interpretation fits the idealized character, and it also provides an opportunity for another pointed contrast. Josefa continually yearns for bourgeois comfort and security; Zapata appreciates his comforts, though not to the point of sacrificing his ideals.

This delineation of the character relationships gives some idea of Steinbeck's sizable task in creating a screenplay that condensed a decade of lively action ranging across the Mexican political and geographical landscape. Steinbeck wanted to stay true to historical outlines, but he also wanted to create intense personal drama. The device by which he parallels people close to Zapata with established historical figures helps achieve both purposes. However, he is forced to seize on a few symbolic incidents and through careful patterns of imagery to link them in a unified whole. At the center of his plot is the maturation of Emiliano Zapata. From the outset Zapata is a formidable figure, but not a man committed to a vision; at the conclusion he is shown as the leader of the people in an almost mystical sense. This development divides itself into three parts which recall the tripartite journey of the Joads in *The Grapes of Wrath*. In the first major section, events impel Zapata to become the leader; in the second, he experiences the temptations of power and success; in the third section, he rejects them and occasions his own sacrificial death.

For the most part Elia Kazan's film lives up to Steinbeck's excellent screenplay. Kazan's major deviations from it are in terms of scenes cut, and some of these omissions are readily understandable as *Viva Zapata!* was for the time a long movie (113 minutes)—even without these additional scenes. Several small cuts seem to have been made in terms of the production code—for example, Pancho Villa's crude jokes about women in his part of the country and Eufemio's about women in his. Essentially only two excisions are really important—the opening scene of Zapata on the white horse and the attempt on his life by Soldadera. In fact, the cutting of scenes which dramatize Fernando's plot against Zapata probably strengthens the final section of the story. Other changes are minor and mostly involve sharpening the dialogue. For example, when Fernando first arrives among Zapata's band the screenplay has him say, "This is all very confusing." In the film, he comments, "This is all very disorganized."

Essentially a film director of literary bent, Kazan came to Hollywood from the New York stage, and has since published several novels: *America, America,* (1962), *The Arrangement* (1967), *The Assassins* (1972). Born in Istanbul in 1909, Elia Kazanjoglou moved with his Greek family to Berlin and later to the United States, where his uncles had already established a rug business. Kazan graduated from Williams College in 1930, attended Yale Drama School in 1931 and 1932, and then apprenticed at the Group Theatre under Lee Strasberg and Harold Clurman in 1933. He directed his first play in 1934, and later made a name for himself with Group Theatre left-wing productions. Like most American leftists he became progressively disillusioned with Stalinist politics both in the Group Theatre and in international relations. His Broadway production of Thornton Wilder's *The Skin of Our Teeth* (1942) brought him to the attention of Hollywood, and 20th Century-Fox called on him to direct *A Tree Grows in Brooklyn* (1945) from the best-selling novel by Betty Smith. Later he directed social film dramas for Darryl Zanuck— *Gentleman's Agreement* (1948) and *Pinky* (1949)—while commuting to New York—"a two coast genius"—to direct strong Broadway fare—Arthur Miller's, *All My Sons* (1947) and *Death of a Salesman* (1949), and Tennessee Williams's *A Streetcar Named Desire* (1947). (His film version of the Williams play appeared in 1951.)

Marlon Brando had achieved stardom under Kazan's direction in *A Streetcar Named Desire,* and the director was able to convince producer Zanuck to use the mercurial young star. Brando had yet to establish his screen personality, and he made his creation of Zapata one of his most memorable roles. Looking back at the film after almost three decades, we can see that some of Brando's typical mannerisms are evident, but the actor subdues the tricks and pranks which so often blur his later roles. (A comparison of his role as the protagonist of *One-Eyed Jacks* [1961], which directed himself, demonstrates the sloppy excesses to which Brando descended when he didn't have firm direction.) By and large the audience forgets Marlon Brando the actor and appreciates Emiliano Zapata the man. An excellent make-up job even recreated the physical image of Zapata. He was the perfect choice for Steinbeck's Zapata, and his performance won him an Academy Award nomination for Best Actor. (He lost to popular favorite Gary Cooper in *High Noon.)*

Kazan also drew a fine performance, perhaps his best, from screen veteran, Anthony Quinn. Quinn was of Mexican background, and he probably found the role of Eufemio a pleasant change from the stereotyped Mexicans he generally played. His performance in *Viva Zapata!* not only won him as Oscar for Best Supporting Actor, but led to the stronger films of his later career, such as Fellini's *La Strada* (1956). An equally fine job was Joseph Wiseman's interpretation of Fernando. Wiseman was to become best known for *Dr. No* (1963) in the James Bond series, but in this film he is able to project a more subtle fanaticism, a fine balance of inhuman strength and cruel weakness. Lou Gilbert, proves almost as good as Pablo, the other contrasting figure for Zapata. Fay Roop as Diaz, Harold Gordon as Madero, Frank Silvera as Huerta, and Alan Reed as Villa all bear uncanny physical resemblances to the historical figures, and all four do very well with their small roles. The only major problem, as several reviewers pointed out, is one that still plagues Hollywood: indifferently done accents. Brando attempts the eloquent simplicity of Steinbeck's "translated Spanish"; Quinn speaks like "a movie Mexican"; while several others sound closer to the state of New Jersey than the state of Morelos. Jean Peters attempts no accent at all as Josefa, which is just as well for this perennial starlet captures nothing essential in the character she impersonates and is the single, unfortunate Hollywood touch in the screen casting.

Viva Zapata! is Kazan's most cinematic film; its epic plot and action are the stuff of movies not the stage.[11] Producer Zanuck probably deserves a good deal of credit for the overall filmic vision, as he did with Ford's *The Grapes of Wrath*.[12] Kazan's sense of authenticity and realism was sharpened on his trips to Mexico, where he and Steinbeck researched the story of the revolution. The music was created from authentic Mexican mariachi tunes recorded by Kazan during his Mexican visits.[13] He also mentions a photographic history of the revolution as a major source, and even tells how he replicated a specific photographic portrait of Zapata, Villa, and other generals.[14] Asked by an interviewer if he was influenced by Eisenstein's *Que Viva Mexico!*, Kazan specifically rejected the idea, saying "the stationary, passive style" of that work was not appropriate for *Viva Zapata!*[15] Instead Kazan posits the influence of Dovzhenko and Eisenstein's films of the Russian Revolution in his own depiction of mass action. His long shots across landscapes he attributes to John Ford, the master of the Western and director of *The Grapes of Wrath*. Kazan had worked with Ford at 20th Century-Fox and said of him, "I got more from Ford than anyone else."[16]

Kazan has called *Viva Zapata!* his first film "that was structurally cinematic," in other words "held together by a frame that is essentially cinematic."[17] The essential framework is Steinbeck's three-part plot, into which a number of small scenes are fitted as in a mosaic. These scenes are realized filmically as well as dramatically in compositions that are both realistic in their recreation of historical sources and symbolic in their implications. The viewer is struck, for example, by the framing of Zapata within the lines of weapons like machine guns, and the use of framing devices inherent in the scene—doors, windows, binoculars—to symbolically focus the action. Kazan makes effective use of composition angles, particularly in visualizing Zapata's rise and fall. (For example, at the conclusion, the camera looks down on Zapata's crumpled body from the viewpoint of the soldiers who have shot him from the roof above the courtyard.) Distance is also manipulated effectively, as in the scene in which Zapata is freed from the *rurales* by the crowd; Kazan keeps cutting back and forth from the landscape flooded with white-clothed peasants and a close-up of Zapata, his neck in the noose. The only cinematic weak points are a penchant for symbolic close-ups on objects—Madero's watch, Pablo's knife, the crucifix in the church—and for rather obvious uses of montage. The montage effects are often jerky and unbalanced (the death of Innocente, for example), not at all like the work of the Russian masters Kazan acknowledges. However, these are small points as against the film's overall visual and dramatic success.

Steinbeck's screenplay opens with the titles backed by the image of "a Man on a White Horse"(3), riding hard across the countryside. After the credits the Man reaches his destination, a rural railroad stop, and the scene switches to the Federal Palace in Mexico City, where he will be identified as Zapata. Unfortunately, in the film the opening scene is replaced by a rather traditional presentation of credits, and the contrast of free country and constricted city is lost. The film's opening scene at the Presidential Palace is still worth considering in detail because it demonstrates Steinbeck's careful use of imagery to unite a number of symbolic scenes. Zapata has joined a group of peasants from his native state of Morelos who have come to the capital to plead with the dictator Diaz to right the wrongs being done them by local landowners. As they enter the Palace, the peasants are searched for weapons, for the most part "long murderous-looking sheath knives"(4). A slight man, later identified as Pablo produces only an inoffensive pen knife; Zapata and the peasants laugh at the contrast. The knife represents the gentle, inoffensive Pablo, who nevertheless has the courage to stand up to Diaz and later to Zapata. When Pablo is executed because of Fernando's plotting, his woman, Soldadera, tries to kill Zapata with the same small knife. When the knife later reappears in close-up, it recalls this scene and crystallizes for Zapata his growing sense that he has become another Diaz.

Many other details in the opening scene function in the

same way. When the peasants are ushered into an audience room they see a magnificent oil painting of the President, a glorious but false image. (Later when Zapata and Villa capture Mexico City, they meet in the same room just as the portrait of Diaz is being unceremoniously carted off.) Diaz greets the peasants as his "children," and generally demonstrates the patronizing attitude suggested in the portrait. At first the others speak, presenting a case against those hacienda owners who have appropriated their land. Diaz concilliates them by saying that the courts will right the matter. As the others turn to leave, the Man asserts the hard fact that the peasants cannot verify the ancient boundaries on land that is fenced and guarded. Diaz is taken aback and asks his name. As he hears the reply, a tight close-up shows the circled name of Emiliano Zapata on a list of the petitioners. Zapata smiles at the implied threat in Diaz's action; he has been singled out from the crowd by word and camera, propelled toward leadership for the first time. Later when Zapata is President, he entertains another group of peasants from Morelos, and another young *charo* confronts him. It is at this exact moment that he rejects the Presidency and returns with them to right the wrongs being perpetrated by his own brother, Eufemio.

The balance of the first section, Zapata's rise to power, contrasts scenes of escalating violence with others of domestic ritual. The juxtaposition of these scenes demonstrates that Zapata is an ordinary man who would have led an ordinary life if leadership had not been continuously thrust upon him. From the Presidential Palace the scene shifts to Morelos where the peasants, led by the Zapata brothers, are marching toward the hacienda fences to establish their ancient rights. When Emiliano orders the fence cut, he has established himself both as a rebel and a leader. The *rurales* attack the peasants, but Emiliano diverts their fire by lassoing their machine gun and pulling it out of the frame. Then he escapes into the mountains where he establishes an outlaw band with Eufemio, Pablo, and few others.

In the next scene Fernando arrives, a messenger from Madero, an exile in the United States planning a revolt against Diaz. The description of Fernando is worth quoting for its careful use of symbolic detail, seen from a symbolic down angle.

He is dressed in rumpled city clothes. He is literally soaked with sweat. He wears a high collar, and boots which come up over his trouser legs. He carries his coat over one arm, a straw hat, and a brief case in the other hand. Hanging from his belt is an 1892 American model typewriter (14).

Fernando describes his typewriter as "the sword of the mind" (16), and he clearly is associated with the ideology of revolution. He reads aloud the speeches he has written for Madero, but Zapata is more interested in a newspaper photo of the man himself. The photo contrasts with the ornate portrait of Diaz, but still Zapata feels that "a picture is only a picture" (20). So he sends Pablo to meet with Madero, while he sets off to woo Josefa. Clearly, the order of these events show that Zapata is a natural leader because he is a natural man and that his leadership is associated with the mountains.

In the next scene Zapata pays court to Josefa in the village church, where he is seen framed with a crucifix. She denies his suit because he has no position nor the hope of any. In exasperation Zapata reveals that he has been offered a pardon and his old job by Don Nacio, the local *patron*. Zapata accepts the offer to please Josefa, but every aspect of his job demonstrates the fundamental injustice of the system which supports it. On a horse buying trip he sees an estate manager strike a hungry child for stealing a horse's food. In anger, Zapata knocks the man down, and only Don Nacio keeps him from killing the oppressor. At this instant, Pablo returns from his meeting with Madero, and Zapata is again confronted by a choice. He temporarily decides in favor of Josefa and bourgeois security, but again events intervene. The group encounters the *rurales* leading a prisoner, old Innocente, along the road with a noose about his neck. Zapata intervenes and the *rurales* panic, dragging the prisoner to his death as they ride off. When Zapata cuts the rope to save the old man, he has committed another act of rebellion. This act leads to his arrest when he goes to Josefa's father to ask for her hand. Soon Zapata is walking down another dusty road, surrounded by *rurales*, with his head in a noose. Then the people gather from all sides—in a neat montage of varying angles and distances—and intimidate the captain of the *rurales* into freeing Zapata. Fernando urges him to destroy the telegraph wire, and when he orders Eufemio to cut it, the captain screams, "This is rebellion!"

At this point in the screenplay, Steinbeck contrasts these scenes with a dinner party at Don Nacio's and a lengthy discussion of the Zapata rebellion. The scene was cut from the final version of the film (though it may have been shot as some of the parts were cast), probably to move the action along. And move it does, as three montaged attacks—on an army patrol, an armored train, and a fortified town—indicate the growing strength of Zapata's forces. As the revolutionary and his men rest in the square of the captured town, Zapata is introduced to a boy who has lassoed an enemy machine gun, putting it out of action. He offers the boy a reward, and the child asks for the white horse, Blanco. Just as Zapata gives away the horse, Fernando arrives with a commission from Madero making Zapata the General of the Armies of the South. Zapata has established his worldly success and political power, but the symbol of his natural power has been passed on to a young follower.

In recognition of this success, Josefa's father asks the new general if he intends to continue courting his daughter. The courting scenes which follow again show Zapata's sensitive, human side, as well as the temptations of bourgeois security. When the Diaz regime falls, Zapata finally is able to marry Josefa, hoping to settle down to an ordinary life at last.

However the power he has assumed requires that Zapata act for the people with the new government in Mexico City. His interview with President Madero replicates the film's

opening scene. Madero is clearly sympathetic with the peasants, but he temporizes, promising that the new "constitu-
tional" courts will handle the problem. Zapata is suspicious,
but he promises to disarm his irregular army and wait for the
operation of democracy. Another force influences the action
at this point, as the cynical General Huerta takes control of
the army and tries to crush the other generals—including
Zapata. Instead of peace, another, more vicious civil war
ensues. This part of the film, like the earlier action of the
revolution, is a montage of battle scenes—the *Zapatistas* arm
and ambush a federal column; the *Federales* counterattack
and execute President Madero in a powerful scene lit by car
headlights and punctuated by car horns and rifle shots.

The most important scene involves Pablo and Fernando,
who represent two sides of Zapata's own personality. Pablo
has still been trying to establish contact with Madero, and to
convince Zapata to ally himself with the gentle liberal.
Fernando accuses Pablo of consorting with the enemy, and
virtually forces Zapata to execute his old friend in order to
enforce discipline on the rank and file. Before his death Pablo
appeals directly to Zapata. "Can a good thing come from a
bad act? Can peace come from so much killing?"(86), he asks.
Pablo's death coincides with the collapse of Huerta's army,
and Zapata returns to Josefa in the hope of enjoying the peace
which is seen as having been dearly bought. As he sleeps, he is
attacked by Soldadera who wields Pablo's little knife. In the
screenplay, when he sees the knife, tears come to his eyes and
we are reminded of the scene which opened the film. Unfortunately, the final print excised the scene of Soldadera's
attack, an important component in the series of scenes which
lead directly to Zapata's renunciation of power.

In a short scene, Pancho Villa establishes Zapata as
President, but Zapata quickly resigns when he finds himself
playing the role of Diaz, circling the name of his critic for
retribution. He returns to Morelos to correct the injustices
which Eufemio has worked in his absence and to lead his

private life. Eufemio has been corrupted by his power and
made cynical by war and killing. Alcohol and adultery are his
only solace now, and to support his vices he has stolen the
land from the people. Before Zapata can help him, the jealous
husband of one of his women guns Eufemio down. In a
moving speech, Zapata tells the people what they must do
now—without a leader.

"About leaders. You've looked for leaders. For strong
men without faults. There aren't any. There are only little
men like yourselves. They change. They desert. They die.
There's no leader but yourselves"(104).

The final section of the story is much shorter than the
first two. In the first part considerable time was taken to
show Zapata impelled to leadership; in the second, less time
is used to show him disillusioned by power. In the third
section, Zapata has already become what he will always be.
His earlier decisions to take power and then to relinquish it
have made him the spiritual leader of the people. Steinbeck
simply shows him living in the mountains, much as he did
after his first brush with the law.

Josefa is with him, and though she complains about
living like an Indian, their love is obviously deep and true.
Against these scenes Steinbeck counterpoints the government's machinations against Zapata. Now these forces are led
by Fernando, who for the first time wears the uniform of a
general.

In the final scene Zapata is lured to a ruined hacienda
with the promise of guns and ammunition from a renegade
general. In actuality Fernando has designed this trap, down
to the bait—Blanco, Zapata's lost white stallion. Distracted
by the reunion with his horse, Zapata lets his guard fall for a
moment, and the trap is sprung. He is cut down by a fusillade
from what seems a whole regiment of soldiers hidden on the
roof. Zapata's crushed body is shown from an extreme down
angle; in death he assumes a helpless fetal position. However,
when Fernando emerges from the shadows to inspect the

body, the white stallion bolts and escapes. Aware that the peasants will make much of this fact, Fernando orders the horse shot, but it escapes. In order to counter rumors, Fernando has Zapata's body dumped in the marketplace, where all can see for themselves that their leader is dead. The women begin to wash his body for burial, and now the body recalls Christ's in a pietà. A veteran of Zapata's army looks at the mangled corpse and asserts that it is not their leader; the others take up the chorus and whisper that Zapata is alive in the mountains awaiting the need of the people. Steinbeck's last image symbolically asserts the spiritual freedom Zapata has achieved even in death; a freedom caught in Kazan's filmic image also.

Exterior, A Mountain Slope
Over a rise of MUSIC we see BLANCO, the WHITE HORSE, walking
    up the slope toward the peak. He's all alone grazing peacefully
    . . .
The End   Fade Out (122)

    All in all, Steinbeck and Kazan working together created in *Viva Zapata!* a brilliant film that might well be Kazan's best screen effort—an effort elicited by his interest in the colorful subject, his political vision of the moment, and his personal identification with Zapata. Steinbeck's talents were reawakened for all of the same reasons; he then created his best screenplay and one of his two major literary works of the postwar period. It is a film that can stand with *Of Mice and Men* and *The Grapes of Wrath*.

V. EAST OF EDEN

East of Eden was published in 1952, the same year in which *Viva Zapata!* was released. Steinbeck had been writing his "big California Novel," the work he believed would revive his literary reputation, since the failure of *The Wayward Bus* in

1947. In his new novel, he turned back to the California past of the nineteenth century to retell the tale of the greatest of American Dreams—the dream of Westering. His working title was *Salinas Valley*.

Steinbeck had experimented with this material in some of his earliest writing, notably in *To A God Unknown* and an unpublished novel about his family. In his late forties, he sensed that he had to go back to the beginnings, both of his life and his art, to find his personal and artistic directions once more. Again he utilized regional, local, and family history; again he sought to root his story in his native earth. Though he wrote most of the novel in New York, he made frequent research trips to California.

When the saga of his own family refused to come to life dramatically, Steinbeck changed directions; he created a second family to balance his own. This new family, the Trasks, played out in allegorical terms the biblical struggle inherent in the American Westering enterprise, the settling of a new Eden. Each generation of the Trask family replayed the fall of Adam and Eve, as well as the murder of Abel and Cain. Soon the dramatic history of the Trasks overpowered the original family saga, and in 1951 Steinbeck changed his title to *East of Eden*.[1] He was never able to reconcile the two plot strands, but he stopped worrying about the problem, justifying the two stories as literary counterpoint.[2] By the fall of 1951, he had produced over a quarter of a million words, his longest work by far.

When *East of Eden* was published in 1952, it proved the anticlimax of Steinbeck's writing career. Pat Covici and other editors at Viking had tried to talk Steinbeck into cutting and rewriting, but he refused.[3] *East of Eden* was to be his great work, and he would stand or fall with it. And fall he did. Viking plugged the book as Steinbeck's epic; a few reviewers liked it, and the public bought it. As though challenged by the jacket blurbs, later critics tore it apart. The task proved an easy one, for *East of Eden* is a very weak novel.

As was obvious to Steinbeck's editors, the two central plot strands neither cohere nor maintain interest. The family history never rises above nicely written reminiscence that fails to come artistically alive, while the dark history of the Trasks is melodramatic allegory in which neither the drama nor the symbolism is coherent. The Trasks are cardboard figures, puppets manipulated by their creator to suit his allegorical purposes with no consideration of credibility or motivation. The style is often labored and affected, though not without some good descriptive passages. Intellectually pretentious and simplistic, the novel takes several hundred pages to conclude that humankind is endowed with a free choice between good and evil (though the behavior of most of the characters seems to deny the existence of free will). Finally and most importantly—*East of Eden* is corny. Steinbeck's novel is one with the pseudo-Freudian epics of the 1950s, a sister saga to novels like *Raintree County* (1951), or the plays of William Inge, or the worst of Tennessee Williams.

Nevertheless it became a best seller, and as such it was a sure bet for the movies. Steinbeck's friend Elia Kazan had first crack at it, and he took an option after reading only the galleys. He then negotiated a deal with Warner Brothers, who bought the screen rights in 1953.[4] Steinbeck was to write the screenplay; Kazan would produce and direct. However, Steinbeck later decided that he had already put too much of himself into the novel and that he could not face the task of transforming it for the screen. Kazan then turned to stage and screen adaptor, Paul Osborn, a playwright who had a number of important screen credits. Working closely throughout 1953, Kazan and Osborn cut Steinbeck's monster of a novel down to screen size. Competently condensing and selecting, Osborn provided a finished script which eventually won an Academy Award nomination. The film was shot on the Warners' lot and on location during the summer and fall of 1954. Finished and released in 1955, it was received much as the novel had been: popular reviewers liked it; the public paid to see it; and the more serious critics panned it for much the same reasons they had savaged the novel.

In several ways Kazan's *East of Eden* is superior to Steinbeck's. The novel's major problem is its rambling, diffuse structure. Steinbeck's story stretches from the Civil War to World War I, and from Connecticut to California. After an opening with a description of the Salinas Valley as an American Eden, Steinbeck introduces his two central characters, the representatives of the two central families. Samuel Hamilton—based on Steinbeck's maternal grandfather—is an immigrant from the north of Ireland, whose history is contrasted with that of Connecticut-born Adam Trask, whose father, Cyrus, has remarried and sired a second son, Charles. Cyrus falls into Adamic corruption through chicanery and adultery while his sons play out the Cain and Abel story. When Charles savagely beats Adam, the latter wanders off to the Indian wars. Meanwhile the Hamiltons have crossed the country and settled down in Salinas, where nine children have blessed their marriage. So far so good. Some of this early writing is taut and realistic, and it initially seems that Steinbeck has produced a chronicle of Westering that would probe the moral meaning of the experience.

The introduction of Cathy Ames precipitates the novel's descent into murky allegory. Steinbeck calls her a "moral monster" when he introduces her, and she quickly justifies this qualification by murdering her parents and apprenticing herself in a whorehouse. Succeeding in her chosen profession, Cathy betrays her procurer—who has inexplicably fallen in love with her—and she is beaten almost to death by the rejected pimp. Adam finds her half-dead, nurses her back to health, and for no apparent reason promptly falls in love with her: Adam needs his Eve.[5] While she is still weak enough to be compliant, Adam takes Cathy to the Salinas Valley of California where he plans an ideal ranch to house his growing family: Cathy has given birth to twin boys who are symbolically named Caleb and Aron. Not cut out for the domestic life,

Cathy soon departs—after shooting Adam so that he can't follow her. However, she only travels as far as Monterey where she finds employment in her old line of work under a new name, Kate. In short order, she poisons the madam and takes over herself, running the kinkiest cat house west of the Mississippi. It seems obvious that Steinbeck was exorcising his anger with his first two wives in his portrait of Cathy/Kate. She becomes the archetypal "Queen Bee bitch" so prevalent in the novels and films of the 1940s and 1950s.

Meanwhile the Hamiltons have gone along with their humdrum lives, only occasionally aware of the Trasks. Samuel is distantly friendly with Adam, but the elder Hamilton soon dies off. Adam then takes his boys and moves into the town of the Salinas, where he raises them with the help of his Chinese cook, Lee. Here they grow up in the neighborhood Steinbeck knew as a child—Olive Hamilton having married Ernest Steinbeck and given birth to John and his sister. In town, the Trask boys both fall in love with vivacious Abra Bacon, while Adam loses his fortune trying to perfect refrigerated produce transportation. When the boys are about sixteen, Cal, the wild son, finds out about his mother, visits her in Monterey, and unsuccessfully tries to inform his father of her existence. The priggish Aron is now engaged to Abra, who really loves Cal. Kate is having troubles also, as one of her whores and her pimp suspect her of having murdered the original madam.

At this point in the saga, the United States enters World War I, and Cal makes a killing in bean futures with money borrowed from Kate. This fortune, made with the help of one of Hamilton's sons, Will, is to buy his father's love with the money lost earlier in the refrigeration gamble. The contrast is obvious; Adam had lost his money in a visionary enterprise, Cal makes his in a corrupt system that cheats the farmers. When Adam naturally rejects the gift, Cal revenges himself not on Adam, his moral father, but on his brother, Aron, confronting him with Kate, their fallen mother! Aron runs away to enlist in the army and to escape his disillusionment. In short order Kate commits suicide; Aron is killed at the front; and Adam has a fatal stroke. However, Abra has revealed her love to Cal, and this somehow changes him, leading to a reconciliation with his father. Adam's final benediction just before his death is the revelation to Cal that he has the power of free will to choose good or evil in his future. Cal's name tritely stands for California, the embodiment of the American Adam in a fallen Eden, but with a chance at redemption.

Justifiably concluding that so unwieldy a plot could not be transformed to the screen, Kazan and Osborn chose to focus on the conflict of Cal and Aron for the love of Adam and of Abra. Though Adam Trask had been the central figure of the novel, the film centers on Cal, the more active of the twins, while Adam becomes a kind of God-like background figure. This change also pushed Cathy/Kate into the background, and the screenwriter wisely dropped all of the evil machinations at the whorehouse. The Hamiltons are essentially cut out of the film, while Lee, the Trasks' philosophical Chinese cook is completely omitted. Certain events are developed, transposed, or dropped in order to give the new central conflict more dramatic focus: much more is made of Cal's gift to his father and its rejection, while Adam's fatal stroke occurs when Aron leaves for the army. Neither Aron nor Kate is dead at the end of the film. Given Kazan and Osborn's stage background, it seems natural that they should have arranged Steinbeck's material into a series of dramatic confrontations organized around an obvious conflict. In many ways this strategy improves on Steinbeck's unwieldy plotting, but it places great importance on casting.

Kazan's dramatic sense also determined his casting of the film. Seeing Cal as the dramatic center of the work—passionate, inarticulate, frustrated—Kazan wanted a "Brando" for the role, but Marlon Brando was unavailable and would in any case have been too mature. Osborn had seen an unknown young actor who reminded him of the mercurial Brando; he arranged a meeting with Kazan and James Dean was discovered for the movies.

Dean's performance is in a sense the pivotal element in the film. He was an instant sensation, guaranteeing the box-office success of the movie, but his Brandoesque histrionic excesses are symbolic of the overdone, arty, inauthentic quality of the whole. Many of the film's contemporary reviewers complained about Dean in these terms, and it is impossible not to agree with them after viewing the film today. Nevertheless *East of Eden* won Dean an Academy Award nomination for Best Actor (he lost to Ernest Borgnine for the title role in *Marty*) and established the personna which made him a cult hero for disaffected youth in the 1950s. After two similar roles in the aptly titled *Rebel Without A Cause* (1955) and in *Giant* (1955), he was killed in a racing car accident—a symbolic death which solidified his cult status.

With the changed emphasis on the brotherly conflict and the absence of other characters, Abra's part in the proceedings becomes much more important. Unfortunately, Julie Harris's interpretation of the girl exists somewhere between the cute tomboy she made her movie debut with in *The Member of the Wedding* (1953) and the hysterical heroines she would later portray in films such as *Reflections In a Golden Eye* (1967). Richard Davallos as Aron completed the romantic triangle. Like Dean and Harris, he was a relative unknown and tended toward similar frantic overacting—from which he was saved only by the fact that his part really gave him little to work with. Raymond Massey, though suitably cast as Adam, was, however, so distant and stoical that he seemed to be still doing *Abe Lincoln in Illinois* (1939). A stage veteran in her screen debut, Jo Van Fleet won the Oscar for Best Supporting actress for her striking portrayal of Kate, and Burl Ives as Sheriff Quinn gave some indication of his later performances in *Desire Under the Elms* (1958) or *Cat On a Hot Tin Roof* (1958).

The production has some good filmic qualities, though many aspects could be stronger. Art Director James Bavasi and Malcolm Bert created realistic interiors, particularly at Kate's whorehouse. Ted McCord's Cinemascope color photography is perhaps the best feature, particularly in beautiful location-shot outdoor sequences. A Hollywood regular with a reputation for cranky brilliance, he had served as cinematographer on a number of fine films including John Huston's *The Treasure of the Sierra Madre* (1948).[6] *East of Eden's* stylistic excesses—the frequent tilts, pans, and skewed close-ups—are more directly attributable to Kazan, who by his own admission was experimenting with camera style.[7] Though the visual style is sometimes effective, as in the use of the wide frame in outdoor scenes; it too often calls attention to itself for no thematic reason. The best scenes involve the confrontation between Adam and Cal over the ill-gotten money, but even here the expressionist use of oblique lines and angles seems strained, more appropriate to a Gothic thriller. The Expressionism of style only calls attention to the unrealistic excesses of characterization and plot. The same is true of sound, which had been used very effectively in *Viva Zapata!* Here it is expressionistically overdone, as at the carnival sequence, or when the train whistle shrieks incessantly, at Aron's departure. Music also proves disappointing; Leonard Rosenman's score is for the most part stock Hollywood accompaniment.

Nevertheless, if in the final analysis *East of Eden* fails to come off as a film, the blame must be traced to the unrealistic, unmotivated, unfocused characters inherited from Steinbeck's novel. Cut off from the development in the earlier parts of the novel, the film's people are even harder to fathom, and popular Freudian bromides of the 1950s substitute for realistic motivation. The clichés of the reviewers give a good sense of these psychological simplicities: ". . . a deeply disturbing insight into what psychologists call the feeling of rejection";[8] ". . . a child who is not loved cannot possibly grow up";[9] "this sibling conflict shows the importance of love."[10] Steinbeck's novel had an underlay of this fashionable hokum; remember that he was the "bachelor" father of two young sons at the time he wrote the book, and was probably absorbing the child psychology of the day. Like so many filmic and literary works of the decade, the film explains away all behavior in popular psycho-jargon. What causes poor Cal's problems? Rejection. What will cure his problems? Love. If we miss the point, Abra spells it all out in her final speech to the stroke-blighted Adam Trask.

Though Kazan may have somewhat improved Steinbeck's *East of Eden*, we need only to look ahead to his treatment of Tennessee Williams's *Baby Doll* (1956) or William Inge's *Splendor In the Grass* (1961) to see why this movie is nevertheless mediocre. Essentially, Steinbeck received the adaptation he deserved. As both a novel and a film, *East of Eden* testifies to the failure of his artistic vision in the postwar period; his documentary and realistic insight into America had given way to pretentious allegory and pop psychology.

Nothing demonstrates Steinbeck's failure of perception better than his remarks about *East of Eden* as novel and film. Rationalizations of the novel's excesses are strewn throughout his *Journal of a Novel: The East of Eden Letters* (1969). His judgments of the film can be found in the program Warner Brothers prepared for the movie premiere in 1955. Acknowledging the changes from the novel, he notes:

> Kazan has not translated my novel "East of Eden" to the screen. He has transferred the story from one medium to another. The picture is not like the book, but, in a larger sense, the picture is the book.[11]

And how does he evaluate the movie version?

> I am asked whether I like the motion picture "East of Eden." I more than like it. I am more than glad that my book has contributed, among all the other contributions, to what is probably the best motion picture I have ever seen.[12]

Even allowing for studio hype, this is an incredible assertion. Had Steinbeck forgotten *Of Mice and Men, The Grapes of Wrath,* and *Viva Zapata!?*

Fortunately for the film, Elia Kazan seems to have remembered the lyrical realism of these earlier films. He also seems to have been aware of the inherent melodrama in Steinbeck's *East of Eden,* and he tried to balance it with an often effective realism of surface detail. Much of the film was shot on location in Salinas and Mendocino, a northern California coastal town which stands in for Monterey at the time of the novel. (An elaborate set recreating Salinas during World War I was built at the Warner studio in Burbank.) The opening of the film provides a good example of Kazan's scenic realism, as it juxtaposes shots of the California coast with Mendocino reconstructed to suggest Monterey in 1917, the time and place announced by titles.

The film opens, significantly, with Cal, not Adam Trask. Cal is the center of Kazan's *East of Eden,* and from the outset he is engaged in the search for love that motivates him throughout the film. Cal has discovered that Kate, the cruel Monterey madam, is in reality his lost mother, Cathy. Though drawn to her, he is characteristically unable to reveal his identity.

Instead he follows Kate along the streets of Monterey as she makes her daily rounds. Kazan tracks the madam with a long following shot that establishes her relationship to the community, and then he pans to Cal on the opposite sidewalk watching and waiting. Dean is very good in these opening scenes, playing very well against Jo Van Fleet as Kate.

When Kate enters the local bank, Kazan's camera stays with her, creating byplay between Kate and Sally, the madam of another "sporting house." Cal lingers outside, and Kazan crosscuts between his central pair. As Kate leaves the bank, a shot establishes her view of Cal leaning against a building, an American flag balancing him in the wide frame.

Cal is clearly the incarnation of California, the prototype of the American Eden.

This proves a fallen Eden, however, as we learn when Kate walks down shabby alleyways toward the row of seedy Victorian piles that have become brothels for the fishing fleet. Lewd remarks from the other houses fail to distract her, though they clearly upset Cal. Kate enters her rather Gothic establishment, leaving Cal the object of Madam Sally's amusement. Again Kazan cuts between the darkened interior of Kate's and the bright sunlit exterior, the street between the houses now paced nervously by Cal. Point-of-view shots show Cal framed in Kate's window, as she sends her bouncer, Joe, to chase the boy away. A series of two-shots depict the more natural relationship between Cal and Sally, a bovine, maternal figure. Finally, Cal entrusts her with his message for Kate. "Tell her, I hate her."

A short scene of Cal atop a freight train, huddling and shivering in the cold as he returns to Salinas, separates the film's first important sequences. The opening in Monterey established Cal's separation from his mother; next a long sequence in Salinas demonstrates his tensions with his father. The sequence opens with Cal, Abra, and Aron walking from school to the icehouse which Adam Trask has purchased to begin the refrigerated transportation of produce. Throughout this sequence Cal's tensions with his parent figures are replayed on another level with Abra and Aron. Kazan underlines the Freudian implications of the scene by visually associating Aron with Adam, and Abra with the lost Cathy. Abra is the only person Cal can talk with about his mother because she recognizes in herself some of Cathy's wildness.

The casting problems of the film became more apparent in this scene as the byplay between the three young people proves nearly unbelievable. Dean's acting limitations are much more obvious in the scenes with the other teenagers than they were in those with the adults in Monterey. In addition, he does not work well with Raymond Massey as Adam. Kazan evidently promoted hostility between the two actors in an example of "method" motivation. Somehow the trick seems to have backfired, creating in both an over-simplified caricature of both their roles.[13]

At the icehouse Adam talks with Will Hamilton (Albert Dekker) and Aron romances Abra, while Cal is left to his own devices. Adam ignores Cal's seconding of Will's advice to forget the icehouse and invest in nonperishable crops like beans. In the same way, Aron scorns Cal's attempts to impress Abra. Again, Kazan plays inside and outside the building, creating some beautiful images in half-light between the huge walls of ice. In fact, the ice becomes symbolic of the emotional chill of Cal's life. In the climax of the scene he attacks the ice itself, sending dozens of huge blocks cascading down the chute toward the others in a symbolic demonstration of his feelings about them. Kazan shoots this action from low angles, capturing the sense of separation represented here. However, the scene sounds better than it plays, and in Dean's performance Cal's irrationality quickly deteriorates into adolescent petulance.

Dean's overwrought acting is matched by overdone camerawork in the next scene, a confrontation in the Trask parlor. After a nightly Bible reading Adam demands, "Why did you push the ice?" Cal moans, "I don't know." The pair are separated by wide-screen distances, tortuously skewed angles, and sickening green colors. Forced to read again from Psalms, Cal performs lifelessly, sending Adam into a rage. Cal then hints at his knowledge of his mother, identifying himself with her. Finally, he storms out into the night—the "rebel without a cause."

Another scene atop a freight train returning to Monterey provides transition to the next important sequence—Cal's confrontation with Kate. With cover provided by a company of Stanford fraternity boys, he gains entrance to the whorehouse, where he prowls the dark corridors in search of his mother's room. A young servant girl, who resembles Abra in her concern for Cal, warns him off, insisting that Kate will have him beaten, perhaps killed. Cal nevertheless forces her to point out Kate's room, and he enters, discovering the aging whore asleep in her chair, her hands twisted like claws in her lap. As he kneels before her, she comes awake screaming in fear and hate. Her cries bring Joe the slugger, who follows Kate's orders to "put the boots" to the boy.

When Cal comes awake he is at the county jail with Sheriff Sam Quinn in attendance. Burl Ives's role here absorbs much of Sam Hamilton's in the novel as he dispenses practical advice and homespun philosophy. Wise in the ways of the world, he warns Cal of the destructive course he has taken in trying to reach his mother. Dean then goes through more adolescent gyrations in response to these pontifications.

The Sheriff saves Cal a train ride by driving him back to Salinas, but the same Southern Pacific steam engine that had hauled Cal earlier now reappears in scenes centering on the first shipment of refrigerated lettuce. The idea has become a fixation for Adam, an attempt to revive his lost dream of California's bounty extended to the world. Abra and Aron are enthusiastic, but it is Cal who provides practical help by stealing a coal chute to load the railroad cars. These location shots of the panoramic Salinas Valley make effective use of the wide screen to suggest the scope of the California dream.

While Adam and Will Hamilton fret about loading the train, Cal flirts with Abra among the corn flowers. Again the setting is beautiful, but the acting is as embarrassing as Abra's bromides about love and loneliness. Later Aron arrives to complete the triangle, and to revenge himself on Cal by telling about the stolen coal chute. The first train of lettuce departs for the East with bands playing, and optimism encourages Adam to buy a car from Will Hamilton in a comedy scene that is soon balanced by the news that the train has stalled in the mountain passes—the produce has spoiled.

Adam takes his loss philosophically, but Cal sees this

reverse as a chance to prove his love and support for him. First, he talks Will Hamilton into taking him on as a partner in his bean futures scheme. Next, he hops a freight back to Monterey and again confronts Kate, this time revealing that he is her son. The scene in Kate's sitting room replays Cal's confrontation with his father in its wide-screen two-shots, severely skewed angles, and bilious colors. But Dean and Van Fleet relate well, and their dramatic business with tea cups and cigarettes almost overcomes the visual pretentiousness of the scene. Cal gets on so well with Kate that she lends him $5000 to finance his investment in beans.

The scene now shifts back to Monterey for the declaration of World War I, announced by the visual cliché of the newspaper headline. The details of California's patriotic fervor prove just as uninspired as the studio sets used for these scenes. The only surprise is that the Trask boys are little affected by the war fever; Aron is morally opposed to combat, while Cal cares only for his beans and his scheme to win his father's love. Adam meanwhile has become chairman of the local draft board, taking his war effort very seriously. A minor theme in the novel, the antiGerman hysteria engendered by World War I, receives a good deal of emphasis in the film— perhaps because it gives Cal's energy some focus in support of his neighbor, old Mr. Albrecht (Harold Gordon). Unfortunately, the defense of Albrecht's house from a ragtag mob proves rather corny, as does Cal's later romp through his burgeoning fields.

The nadir of the film is reached in the next sequence, a long evening in the local amusement park. Something of a set piece in films of the 1950s, scenes of fairs generally represented a gaudy microcosm of the general culture. Here the fair functions as a sort of fairyland in which Cal and Abra can find love. She is separated from Aron for the evening, and Cal soon abandons his date for her. They ramble through all the requisite fun of the fair—crazyhouse, candystand, ferris wheel. Later a mechanical failure suspends them along high above the earth on the ferris wheel. They kiss for the first time, and their romantic fate is sealed.

The mood changes as a propaganda speech by a visiting soldier soon turns into another raid on old Albrecht. Cal leaves Abra atop the ferris wheel and climbs down in time to defend the old man from attack. The ensuing free-for-all is finally stopped by Sheriff Quinn and his deputies, but not before Mr. Albrecht's home is wrecked. Aron arrives and, disguising his resentment of Abra's attention to his brother, accuses Cal of starting all the trouble. He attacks Cal with his fists, and after their fight Cal goes off to get drunk, while Aron returns home to report on Cal. The drunken Cal later visits Abra, and in a scene that extends their romance in Romeo and Juliet terms by climbing a tree to her window.

Cal must be reconciled with his father before he can fulfill his love for Abra. Accordingly, he plans a birthday party for Adam at which he will replace the money his father lost on the lettuce venture. Again Dean descends to adolescent foolery as Cal and Abra decorate the house for the party. Adam, preoccupied by his decisions at the draft board, hardly acknowledges the festivities until Cal shocks him with the hefty package of greenbacks. Aron, not to be upstaged, announces his engagement to Abra. Though she has not been consulted, Abra feels compelled to second Aron in this circumstance. Adam then accepts Aron's "gift" but refuses Cal's. The father sees it as tainted money, war profits. Doubly rejected, Cal turns on Aron, revealing their mother's whereabouts and current profession. The scene is the dramatic center of the film, a montage of wild angles, colors, and sound effects.

A quick trip to Monterey results in a confrontation between Aron and Kate. This time it is Aron who goes off to get drunk, while Cal returns for another sharply angled confrontation with his father. Now Cal reveals his knowledge of Cathy/Kate to Adam, insisting that he is her son not his. Next Sheriff Quinn arrives with word that Aron has enlisted in the army and is leaving on the next train. At the station, just as the troop train departs, they all meet in time to receive Aron's drunken curse. Adam then collapses with a stroke.

The film's final scenes take place in Adam's room, where he lies paralyzed. Abra nurses him, and a contrite Cal returns to seek his father's pardon and blessing. Adam seems to reject him again, and Cal runs off only to be stopped by the Sheriff. Meanwhile Abra talks to Adam urging him to forgive Cal before it is too late. Again her lines about the power of love are too unbelievably florid. However, if they fail to convince us, they do move Adam, who delivers a biblical sermon on man's ability to choose between good and evil. Finally, he extends his hands in benediction. Cal and Abra are united now in the love of Adam, who peacefully composes himself for death.

This conclusion leaves a number of loose ends, notably Kate and Aron, who are both dead at the end of the novel. However, the theme of the film is so banal, the characterization so inadequate, and the style so pretentious, that plot difficulties pale in comparison. The 1950s simplicities about love and loneliness are reminiscent of William Inge plays like *Picnic*, (filmed in 1956) and *Splendor In the Grass* (filmed in 1961 by Kazan). This is "Literature" Hollywood-style, Literature with a capital L. Unfortunately, this fashionable silliness came not from some hack scenarist but from the novelist himself. Despite the efforts of screenwriter Paul Osborn and director Elia Kazan, the dead weight of Steinbeck's *East of Eden* was simply too much to overcome.

VI. THE WAYWARD BUS

Steinbeck was disappointed by the critical reception of *East of Eden*, and though he masked his feelings of failure with his customary surface bravado,[1] he quickly dropped his plans for a sequel that would have carried the family story up to the present. During a long European trip, he worked on a screenplay of Henrik Ibsen's play *The Vikings*, but abandoned the project in spite of encouragement from Ingrid Bergman.[2] When the novelist returned to New York, composer Frank Loesser contacted him about a musical version of *Cannery Row*.[3] During 1953, Steinbeck worked on a love story for a musical; that story evolved into the novel *Sweet Thursday* (1954), a sequel to *Cannery Row*. Rodgers and Hammerstein finally presented their musical version of the new novel as *Pipe Dream* in 1955. One of their less successful efforts, it was only slightly more silly and sentimentalized than the Steinbeck novel on which it was based. *Cannery Row* itself had been a diversion; *Sweet Thursday* was a blatant effort to cash in on past commercial success.

Sweet Thursday tells how romance came to *Cannery Row*'s Doc in the person of Suzy, another hooker with a heart of twenty-four carat gold. Mack and the boys from the Palace Flophouse are again responsible for the events, which include a wild birthday party for Doc. They know Doc "needs a dame," and giving Suzy "a quick assay" they see "she's the one." Listen to this description: ". . . when she grinned her eyes crinkled"[4] (48). Doc thinks he needs to write a scientific paper on octopi, and he resists their efforts as go-betweens. Yet when Fauna, the new madam at the Bear Flag, dresses Suzy out in a woolen suit, new shoes, clean gloves, and a white handkerchief—how can he resist? Doc's rich pal "Old Jingleballicks" even fixes him up with a fellowship from Cal Tech so that he can write his octopi paper. The wild birthday party, at which the boys dress up as Disney's Seven Dwarfs, temporarily causes a lover's spat, but when Doc's arm is broken by one of the boys, Suzy is all sympathy. At the end they go riding off into the sunset to observe the octopi and presumably to live happily ever after. Even a short summary indicates the basic silliness of the novel; Steinbeck was writing with both the movies and musical comedy in mind, and he was as far as he could be from his original sources of inspiration: documentary realism. *(Sweet Thursday* became part of the 1982 *Cannery Row.)*

Pipe Dream's flop on Broadway prevented it from reaching the screen, but the popular success of *East of Eden* as a movie created a market for film adaptations of Steinbeck works. *Cannery Row* still didn't make it, but *The Wayward Bus* was dusted off for a screen trip. The choice of this ten-year-old novel also was occasioned by the success of *Bus Stop* in 1956, the William Inge play brought to the screen with Marilyn Monroe as the blonde ingenue. The film established Monroe as a major star, and 20th Century-Fox thought a similar bus ride might have the same effect on the career of their blonde bombshell, Jayne Mansfield. Steinbeck had nothing to do with the production so he can be spared the blame for the excesses of the movie. Yet the picture seems of a piece with Steinbeck's work of the period. Although his *The Wayward Bus* (1947) received less than it deserved at the hands of Hollywood in 1957, his overall development was still getting the movie adaptation appropriate to it.

The Wayward Bus had been a modestly successful novel, both in popular and artistic terms. Originally it had seemed somewhat disappointing as Steinbeck's first long book since *The Grapes of Wrath,* but in comparison with later works it appears a modestly honest and competent effort Steinbeck had conceived the novel on his 1945 trip to Mexico in connection with the filming of *The Pearl,* and though he finally set the story in California, it retains some of the ambiance of his Mexican works. The change in settings probably worked to the novel's detriment, as the Mexican landscape would have provided a harsh backdrop against which he could outline his American characters. The American background includes a lot of extraneous detail and social satire that have dated very quickly. In addition, the book needed more polish; it has the raw feeling of a first draft. Convinced that the basic form was still eluding him, Steinbeck had wanted to do extensive revision, but his publisher rushed him into publication for economic reasons. A few years later Steinbeck admitted his mistake in a letter: "A few of the critics saw through *The Wayward Bus* and they were right. It was a paste-up job, and I should have never let it go out the way it did."[5]

The basic structural idea of the novel is sound. As in *The Grapes of Wrath*, Steinbeck employs the journey motif; as in *Lifeboat*, he makes the vehicle a symbolic world; as in *The Pearl* he creates an allegorical frame almost medieval in its complexity. The novel's epigraph is taken from the medieval morality play, *Everyman*.

> I pray you all give audience
> And hear this matter with reverence
> By figure a moral play;
> The summoning of Everyman it is
> That of our lives and ending shows
> How transitory we be all day.

Clearly, Steinbeck implies that he is writing a modern Canterbury pilgrimage, a story which shows human variety against the backdrop of eternity. The novel is laced with religious symbolism. The wayward vehicle belongs to Juan Chicoy (like Jim Casy a Christ-like guide); it travels from Rebel Corners to San Juan de la Cruz (St. John of the Cross); its dashboard bears a metal image of Our Lady of Guadelupe, while front bumper bears the legend in Spanish "the great power of Jesus." Of course, the rough and ready Chicano bus driver because an obvious Christ-figure; the names Rebel Corners (founded by an ex-Confederate family) and San Juan de la Cruz have lost their significance to contemporary Californians; the statue of the Virgin complements a pistol in the glove compartment, and the bumper has been painted over with the vehicle's new name—"Sweetheart." This name proves appropriate, since the major

tensions of the journey are sexual. Steinbeck seems to be
using the eternal verities as a background for his analysis of
contemporary sexual morals.

Because of difficulties in setting, character, and plot the
novel falls short of his goals. The Mexican setting would have
been much better for isolating the characters and creating
tensions. The earthly pilgrimage and the dark night of the
soul suggested by the epigraph and the name of San Juan de
la Cruz are not well realized by a short California bus ride. In
spite of flood and mud, no real tension develops because we
know the characters can always walk to safety. Unlike the
passengers in John Ford's *Stagecoach* (1939), which uses the
same basic device, these voyagers have no reason to risk their
lives. The characters are also somewhat unbelievable within
these surroundings. Why would the wealthy Pritchards be
traveling by a brokendown bus when they could be riding the
Sunset Limited? Once the journey starts improbabilities
mount as events are shaped to the author's symbolic purposes.

Steinbeck could have managed his setting and plot in
allegorical terms if he had created believable characters.
However, as in *Lifeboat* the characters are more types,
selected for purposes of the allegory, than real people. In fact,
as representative types the middle-aged Pritchards elicit long
essays on upper middle-class sexual mores. Mrs. Pritchard's
problems are analyzed down to the intimate details of her
anatomy: her pettiness is caused by a dyspeptic stomach and
a "hooded" clitoris. Pages are spent describing the teenage
sex fantasies of Alice and Kit. Apparently Steinbeck knew he
had created types, and then agonized over them, adding
details to make them seem real.

Although critics objected most strongly to the characterization of Juan Chicoy, the God-like busdriver, he seems in
many ways the strongest characterization of the group.
Perhaps his Mexican background allowed Steinbeck to give
him the characteristics of Kino, the protagonist of *The Pearl*,

or Emiliano Zapata. His virtues are stark and simple, and they don't have to be embellished with a lot of meaningless detail. The others in the novel include: Alice Chicoy, Juan's sloppy American wife; Norma, a star-struck teenage waitress at the Chicoy's truck stop cafe; Kit "Pimples" Carson, Juan's teenaged assistant mechanic, the Pritchards' college student daughter, Mildred; Ernest Horton, an army veteran reduced to selling novelties on the road; Van Brunt, a cranky old man nearing death; and Camille Oaks, the blonde bombshell.

After a long introduction at the truck stop, Steinbeck sets his little group in motion toward San Juan de la Cruz. Relations between Juan and Alice—who does not make the trip but stays home to get drunk—are tense because he is attracted to the comely Mildred Pritchard. The older married couple, are also tense with each other because Mr. Pritchard is obviously smitten by Camille Oaks—as are "Pimples" Carson, Ernest Horton, and even old Van Brunt. Camille, a goodhearted lady of easy virtue in the Steinbeck tradition, befriends only poor Norma. On their way up the flooded canyon, across a weakened bridge, and finally along an old stagecoach track, relations within the group are altered. After the bus gets stuck in the mud, Juan beds Mildred in an abandoned house; the Pritchards make peace sexually; Camille forms a relationship with Ernest; and "Pimples" sees Norma in a new light. As for Van Brunt, he suffers a fatal stroke. Disgusted with his passengers, Juan had intended to abandon them and return to Mexico, but his interlude with Mildred restores his sense of responsibility, and he returns to dig out the bus and drive on. The novel ends as he points out the distant lights of San Juan de la Cruz. We are asked to somehow accept the notion that like the others he has changed and grown after seeing his life as measured against things that never change.

More than any other Steinbeck novel, *The Wayward Bus*[6] makes use of film as a subject. Norma is in love with the screen image of Clark Gable; "Pimples" takes most of his

ideas from the movies; Ernest sells photos of the stars;
Camille looks like a Hollywood starlet; even the Pritchards
react to their precarious position with information and attitudes gleaned from the movies. Only Van Brunt and Juan
are free from the miasmic influences of the Hollywood dream
world; only these two face reality—the one in death, the other
in life. Ironically, Hollywood proceeded to reduce Steinbeck's
modest satire on its pernicious effects into a perfect example
of his complaints. *The Wayward Bus* is not a strong novel, but
it is a perfectly awful movie.

The screenplay for *The Wayward Bus* was done by Ivan
Moffat, a competent screenwriting hand who had scripted
several literate adaptations including *Giant* (1956) from the
Edna Ferber novel for George Stevens, *They Came to Cordura*
(1959) from the Glendon Swartout novel for Robert Rossen,
and *Tender Is the Night* (1962) from the F. Scott Fitzgerald
novel for Henry King. Evidently Steinbeck's advice was
sought, but he took no active part in the writing.[7] Moffat's
screenplay eliminates everything of literary and social value
in the novel. The story's allegorical structure is completely
lost (aside from a few vague religious references and Juan's
dashboard statue) along with the satirical surface detail.
What remains are the bare bones of the plot, the outlines of
the character types, and the California setting. The production seems to have settled on special effects as its strong
point, and more attention is payed to the floods and
mudslides than the interrelationships of the passengers on
this land-borne "ship of fools."

The film characters are reduced to stereotypes even far
more simplistic than Steinbeck's originals. Young, good looking Rick Jason plays "Johnny" Chicoy, the *macho* hero, and
his wife, Alice, is the fetching Joan Collins, heroine of many
exploitation flicks. If the Chicoys are too young and pretty,
Dan Dailey is much too old for Ernest Horton, and the
romance which blossoms with Jayne Mansfield as Camille
seems ludicrous. As an actress, Mansfield's best points were

her natural physical endowments, and in *The Wayward Bus* she gives only a tawdry imitation of Marilyn Monroe. Mildred Pritchard is played by nubile Delores Michaels, and motivation for her fling with Johnny is provided by a broken romance with a basketball coach. Though in the course of the journey romance seems to blossom briefly for them, we eventually learn that Johnny is only interested in making his wife jealous and that Mildred is trying to take revenge on her parents. Though understandably fed up with Alice's drinking, stinginess, and nagging, as he faces death crossing a bridge straining with the flood, he abruptly realizes that he truly loves her. As he announces to Mildred, "When I'm in her arms, I'm the only guy in the world." Meanwhile Alice misses her Johnny, and when the Highway Patrol helicopter stops by for coffee, she hitches a ride to San Juan to greet her husband. They are only one of the neatly paired couples who emerge from the ride. When the wayward bus arrives in San Juan the battling Pritchards are reconciled with each other; Mildred is going back to marry the coach; Van Brunt—who dies in the novel—reveals his reason for haste—marriage to a merry widow; and Kit and Norma are headed for the altar—as are Ernest and Camille despite the fact that he has seen her nudie pictures in *Naked Truth*, a pornographic journal. The tone of this romantic resolution is indicated by Ernest's promise to buy the undomestic Camille a stove which plays "Tenderly" when the meal is cooked. The whole effort smacks more of television's "Love Boat" than *Ship of Fools*, more of "Fantasy Island" than *Everyman*.

The production values are generally bad, except for the special effects. In a doomed effort to salvage the film, director Victor Vicas, a French filmmaker, imposed a turgid visual style on the stereotyped material. Steinbeck's original was straightforward and realistic in style, and Vicas's attempts at expressionism—symbolic close-ups, arty angles, and reflected images—fit neither the Steinbeck nor the Moffat versions of the story. (Vicas was to make only one other American film, an equally muddled spy thriller, *Count Five and Die*, 1958.) 20th Century-Fox's version of *The Wayward Bus* generally looks like what it is—a poor man's *Bus Stop* using John Steinbeck's name above the title. Although Steinbeck cannot be held responsible for the film, it did his waning critical reputation no good. When it opened to universally negative reviews, he was often blamed for this disaster.

VII. FLIGHT AND FINAL WORKS

Steinbeck lived and wrote for more than a decade after the debacles represented by Rodgers and Hammerstein's *Pipe Dream* and Moffat and Vicas's *The Wayward Bus*. During this period he published two novels: *The Short Reign of Pippin IV* (1957) and *The Winter of Our Discontent* (1961); three books of non-fiction: *Once There Was A War* (1958), his World War II dispatches with a new preface, *Travels With Charley* (1961), *America and Americans* (1966), and a considerable number of occasional pieces. A major uncompleted project was a translation of Malory's Arthurian Tales in cooperation with the scholar Eugene Vinauer. At one point Steinbeck called the project "the largest and I hope the most important I have ever undertaken." He seems to have abandoned it after a year's work, leaving some very well written fragments which were published posthumously in 1976. His work also continued to interest other mediums: his early short story "Flight" received a noncommercial film production in 1961; other early stories were dramatized on television series; *Of Mice and Men* was remade as a television feature; *Travels With Charley* and *America and Americans* also appeared on the television screen. Steinbeck continued to make a great deal of money and to garner honors and awards, most notably the Nobel Prize for Literature in 1962.

The Short Reign of Pippin IV is subtitled *A Fabrication*, but Steinbeck's qualifying subtitle was disregarded by reviewers who pounced on this light work as if it were the author's final sellout of his 1930s realism. Stung by the critical failure of *East of Eden*, Steinbeck traveled extensively in Europe and even lived for a time in Paris. His French experience provided a "fabricated" backdrop for a light treatment of American politics. Pippin of the short reign is an unassuming Frenchman elevated to the restored throne of France by a stalemate among the political parties. The intellectual, retiring, witty Pippin seems a portrait drawn from Democratic presidential candidate Adlai Stevenson, the "egghead" of American politics during the 1950s. Stevenson was first a favorite and later a friend of Steinbeck's, and the author deftly satirizes the vapid blankness of the Eisenhower years in his picture of France in the 1950s. To all appearances, he was simply having fun in his first long fiction after the exhausting *East of Eden*.

Elevated to the throne because he is a descendent of Charlemagne, Pippin tries to create a sensible government for his subjects. Of course, the various power blocs both within and without his kingdom are appalled by his common sense liberalism, and Pippin is quickly dethroned. Taken for what it is, *The Short Reign of Pippin IV* is a delightful entertainment with a serious political point. Both this novel and Steinbeck's next were optioned to Hollywood, but neither became a film.

The Winter of Our Discontent (1961), Steinbeck's last novel, seems a serious version of the subjects treated lightly in the satire of French and American politics. The setting here is a small Long Island town, much like Sag Harbor where the Steinbecks had established a permanent home, and the time is the spring and summer of 1960. The real place and time are America and the 1950s: the winter of American discontent. The empty Eisenhower years are here envisioned as a new waste land, a sort of Dust Bowl of the spirit, but though Steinbeck could recreate the moral indignation of his Depression decade novels, he could no longer create the literary structures to match his ideas. As in *The Grapes of Wrath* he focuses on one family, the Hawleys, to represent the awful effect of this American spiritual Depression. However, unlike the Joads, the Hawleys never come alive; they remain stick figures acting out the author's thematic assertions about the Cold War period.

Even Ethan Allen Hawley, the protagonist, remains a sort of moral blur, a man sensitive to the corruptions of his day yet not strong enough to resist them. Though Hawley contemplates bank robbery and adultery, participates in kickbacks and blackmail, he is nevertheless shocked when his son plagerizes an essay to win the "Why You Love America" contest sponsored by the local newspaper. Like Pippin, Hawley is elevated to the leadership of the town in spite of his weaknesses. He contemplates suicide as a way out of his conflicts, but in a complete reversal of mood decides to make things right, to regain his lost legacy of family integrity. Though Steinbeck makes much of the early American background in the town, the place isn't really set anywhere. Rather it has the feel of one of those Frank Capra movie towns which represent a generic America. All the rooting in real place which supports the growth of his best work is missing here. When the Nobel Prize Committee made its award to Steinbeck in recognition of the continuities evident in *The Winter of Our Discontent*, they were right about theme, wrong about structure and style.

More evidence of the changes in Steinbeck's fiction was provided by the film version of "Flight" which was produced in 1961. Written in the early 1930s and later collected in *The Long Valley* (1938), the story is a *tour de force* of naturalism and nonteleolgy, a stark, realistic observation of a deadly chase through the harsh mountains of the Coast Range. Pepe Torres, the *paisano* protagonist, is balanced on the edge of manhood at the age of nineteen. In adolescent self-assertion, he accidently kills a man in a drunken brawl. The dead man's friends then pursue him into the mountains and kill him. As

Pepe is chased he is reduced to the level of an animal, "a wounded beast," yet when he comes to die, his manly courage affirms his real maturation through this primal struggle. Set in California, the story prefigures the harsh realism of Steinbeck's Mexican parables, particularly *The Pearl*. The strength of the story is its documentary presentation of man in the natural world, the closely observed world of the Monterey Coast and the Santa Lucia mountains.

The film succeeds most admirably in recreating this real setting through location shooting. An amateur production made on a shoestring budget, it nevertheless captures Steinbeck's story by remaining true to the reality of spirit, setting, and action. Unfortunately the overall effect is weakened by the characterizations of the amateur cast and the awkward visual style of the young director. While *Flight* cannot be reckoned with the best of the Steinbeck films, it's honest artistic commitment emphasized the importance of Steinbeck's realism and results in an end product more successful than most of the Hollywood adaptation of the writer's works. Evidently, the novelist sensed this bond of artistic kinship, for he not only gave away the film rights but appeared as the narrator to open and close the work.[1]

Flight was the product of a partnership between writer Barnaby Conrad, a Steinbeck friend, and filmmaker Louis Bisbo. When Bisbo approached Conrad with the idea of filming Steinbeck's story, Conrad secured permission from the author and helped raise $90,000 for the venture.[2] Unfortunately, they made a feature length film hoping for theatrical release.[3] The story was padded with long expository sequences, including the café brawl, counterpoint between Pepe and pursuers, and an interpolated sequence about an old man and a girl Pepe meets in the mountains.[4] However, when the film failed to obtain general commercial release, Conrad cut it back to a twenty-minute version closely approximating the short story. Though the California settings and the

Chicano cast look right, director Bisbo never captures the style of Steinbeck's original. Instead of a lyric documentary, *Flight* is a poorly edited chase, often reminiscent of a "B" Western. The music provided by jazz guitarist Laurindo Almeida is considerably stronger than the visual continuity. However, despite its failings, like Steinbeck the audience can appreciate the film's artistic sincerity.

A third Steinbeck work in 1961 was his immensely popular *Travels With Charley*, the narrative of a long motor trip around the United States in the company of his pet poodle, Charles le Chien. Adlai Stevenson had suggested the trip to the ailing Steinbeck as a tonic for his spiritual depression. Evidently it worked, for Steinbeck's viewpoint is immeasurably brighter than in *The Winter of Our Discontent*. Although he recorded the dark side of the American consciousness in his accounts of Southern segregation battles and Northern urban blight, he concludes with a positive vision tied to the inauguration of John F. Kennedy in 1961. *Travels With Charley* contains good reportage, some amusing satire, and some fine writing. Though basically a lightweight work, it provides a pathetic portrait of a querulous old man wheeling aimlessly around the country in a camper with only a neurotic poodle for company.

America and Americans (1966), Steinbeck's last book, is a glossy version of the documentary literary-photographic records of a changing nation popular in the 1930s and 1940s. In it Steinbeck comes to sanguine conclusions unsupported by the facts about the national situation. His narration is a hymn to the American past, a backward look at the spirit that had made America great. Turning resolutely from such discomfiting facts as the American involvement in Vietnam—an involvement he publicly supported—the writer closes his career with a nostalgic rather than a realistic vision of America. Plagued by illness, Steinbeck wrote little in his final years; he died on December 20, 1968.

VIII. TELEVISION

During his later career Steinbeck became interested in the storytelling possibilities of television as well as of film. In 1948, he participated in the formation of a television production company with Robert Capa—his photographer for *A Russian Journal*—and several others, but his own interest in this venture remained more financial than creative.[1] Nevertheless, television's omnivorous appetite for stories and Steinbeck's constant need for money soon combined to bring several of his works to the small screen during his lifetime. Since his death, three of his major fictions have been refilmed as made-for-television movies—*The Red Pony* (1973), *East of Eden* (1981), and *Of Mice and Men* (1981). Along with the belated Hollywood version of *Cannery Row* (1982), they indicate a continuing popular interest in Steinbeck and his fiction. In particular, Robert Blake's television reprise of Lewis Milestone's *Of Mice and Men* demonstrates the artistic potential for the adaptation of Steinbeck's fiction. Although these possibilities have been rarely realized on the small screen, these productions—good and bad—may serve as glosses on the fictions and the films more directly connected with Steinbeck's career.

Television versions of Steinbeck's fiction began with "Molly Morgan," a dramatic adaptation of a chapter from *The Pastures of Heaven*. The story, presented live by the *Nash Airflyte Theater* on December 21, 1950, with Barbara Bel Geddes in the title role, was part of a series of half-hour dramas aired once a week for a thirty-six week season. Understandably, it turned even to the lesser works of traditional writers for materials. "Molly Morgan" proved typical of the treatment Steinbeck received in early television production—respectful, if uninspired.

The most accomplished of television's anthology-type series was CBS's *Omnibus*, a decidedly "high-brow" variation of the type. *Omnibus* treated its mass audience to everything from opera to documentary, from Shakespeare to Saroyan. Steinbeck seems to have been a special favorite of the producers as three of his stories, all adapted from chapters of *The Pastures of Heaven*, were presented in the very first season. These three were: "Nobody's Fool" on January 3, 1954 with veteran character actor Thomas Mitchell; "Nothing So Monstrous" on January 24, 1954 with Lew Ayres (later to appear as Candy in the 1981 television production *Of Mice and Men*) and Tommy Rettig (later to star on the *Lassie* series); "The House" on March 7, 1954 with Buddy Ebsen and Mabel Page. All of these productions were well mounted and well received.

In the same year *Video Theatre*, another anthology series, adapted Steinbeck's earlier story and movie *A Medal For Benny* to a half-hour format, probably improving it in the tightening. It ran on November 25, 1954, featuring J. Caroll Naish (who also starred in the 1945 film) and a youthful Anne Bancroft as the Latin bombshell played earlier by Hedy Lamarr. Television critics complained that the material had dated in the decade since the original film.

A more ambitious use of Steinbeck's Chicano materials was "The Flight," a one hour *Studio One* presentation on June 11, 1956, which added an article to Steinbeck's story title. Unfortunately the taut little story was "fleshed out" with events during Pepe's visit to Monterey, including a musical blessing of the fishing fleet featuring the John Butler Dancers in a routine reminiscent of *The Pearl* filmed in 1947. The 1961 film version proved considerably better as indicated above.

When the live drama anthology passed from television, Steinbeck was less often seen on the small screen. His works returned to the medium on December 3, 1967 with an "NBC News Special" presentation of *America and Americans* narrated by Henry Fonda, the Tom Joad of *The Grapes of Wrath*. Fonda, now a good friend of the author's, was again the host for *Travels With Charley*, another special on March 17, 1968; it featured dramatized and animated action along with documentary footage and background songs by Rod McKuen. These productions were essentially appropriate to their matter; since many of the observations in Steinbeck's *America and Americans* already smacked of a theatrical travelogue, and *Travels With Charley* was nearly as simplistic as Rod McKuen's lyrics.

Steinbeck proved very popular during the television season of 1967–68; between *America and Americans* and *Travels With Charley*, a full-length adaptation of *Of Mice and Men* was broadcast on January 31, 1968. Advertised as a "Movie Special," it was actually a videotaped production of the author's play with a few outdoor shots interspersed. Produced by David Susskind and directed by Ted Kotcheff, the televised work falters between the styles of theater and film. The strange casting of Britisher Nichol Williamson as Lennie simply does not work, nor is the rest of the casting, especially an inexperienced Joey Heatherton as Curly's wife, much better. Another problematic factor is a decidedly homoerotic cast given to the George-Lennie relationship, an emphasis not to be found in Steinbeck's original work.[2] The 1960s reading only confuses the 1930s issues realized so well in Lewis Milestone's earlier film version.

A more thoughtful production of "The Harness," a fine psychological story included in *The Long Valley*, showed on the *World Premiere* of April 15, 1972. It starred Lorne Greene in the central role of a successful farmer psychologically constrained by the "harness" of middle-class morality. The story is one of Steinbeck's most subtle, and the dramatization is memorable for a finer psychology than Greene would achieve in the family conflicts of his *Bonanza* series.

Robert Totten's *The Red Pony*, broadcast on March 18, 1973, was the first made-for-television movie adaptation of a Steinbeck work. In this instance, unlike the *East of Eden* and *Of Mice and Men* in 1981, the television version proceeds directly from the work itself and demonstrates little awareness of the earlier screen version. Since the latter's stock "kid and his horse" treatment was perhaps studio imposed despite the fact that Steinbeck wrote the script, this might have been just as well.

However, Totten's television version not only demonstrates many of the same faults that marred the earlier film, but creates even greater ones in terms of plot and characterization. Most notably, the teleplay excises Billy Buck, evidently in an attempt to focus more directly on the father-son relationship, a change probably occasioned by the star billing of Henry Fonda as Mr. Tiflin. Fonda was a wonderful actor, but he would have been more appropriate as an aging Billy Buck, or as Clint Howard's grandfather rather than as Steinbeck's weak father figure. In this version he is a tough old bird, a sort of throwback to the frontier, trying to make a man of a son sissified by an indulgent mother. The mom is played by Maureen O'Hara, again too old for the role. Ben Johnson, Jack Elam, and Richard Jaeckel are all effective in minor roles that have little or no source in Steinbeck's work but seem drawn from aspects of the missing Billy Buck.

In a few particulars, the television version is equal to the 1949 movie. For example it features location shooting, realistic dialogue, and a graphic view of the birth of a colt, but it timidly sacrifices these advantages to the same cliché happy ending. Nevertheless, the episodic nature of a television movie does allow more incident from the story sequence to be included—Old Gitano's return, for example. All in all, though this story of a rather tense and obviously Oedipal conflict is not without interest in its own right, but it really has little to do with Steinbeck's *The Red Pony*, the finest of his shorter works.[3]

The 1981 television production of *East of Eden* falters because it stays too close to Steinbeck's original fiction. The eight-hour mini-series shown on February 8, 9, and 11 recreates almost all of the Trask family strand from the novel along with a good bit of the Hamilton family material. Because of this faithfulness it inherits the problems of the novel: the plot strands cohere no better in this televised "junker" than in Steinbeck's bloated epic. Moreover, television's interest in the work seems almost prurient, occasioned by the contemporary penchant for a steamy family saga presented in soap-opera style—for example the super popular series *Dallas*, or its Colorado and California clones, *Dynasty* and *Falcon's Crest*. *East of Eden* allowed ABC to mask its lust for easy ratings with Steinbeck's "serious" literary reputation, and the network even mailed educators a study guide to the "philosophical issues" of this blatant ratings grabber.

Wallowing in every trashy or sentimental bit in the original novel and throwing in an odd adultery or abortion for good measure—the production ignores the book's few redeeming elements, and shows none of Steinbeck's nor Kazan's sense of style. Performances are adequate at best, overwrought or underdone at worst. Jane Seymour, an expatriated British actress, was a strange choice for Cathy/Kate. Although a fetching trollop in the early segments, she cannot carry the later importance of her role. Cathy still steals the show, however, becoming the central figure because of the script's emphasis on softcore porn and Timothy Bottoms's self-effacing performance as Adam Trask. He seems such a ninny that the popular audience probably never suspected his "philosophical" role as American Adam. The casting of Sam Bottoms, Timothy's brother, as Cal Trask, provides family resemblance, but at the cost of visual realism as both father, son, *and* Cathy/Kate all are the same age. In fairness, however, it should be said that Sam Bottoms's quieter Cal is a decided improvement over James Dean's histrionics. The rest of the cast is more or less competent and includes Warren Oates as Cyrus Trask, Ann Baxter as his hapless wife, Bruce Boxleitner as Charles Trask, Howard Duff as Edwards, Lloyd Bridges as Samuel Hamilton, and Richard Masur as Will Hamilton. Most of the $11,200,000 production values are little more than adequate, but there is some beautiful Salinas Valley location shooting. The symbolic use of the natural setting when Adam arrives in California remains the one impressive effect of the work. Although director Harvey Hart mounted a handsome production, cinematically it is typical of network television movies: a few nice zoom shots punctuating long stretches of visual tedium heightened only by melodramatic climax.

For the serious student of Steinbeck this television version is interesting primarily because it confirms the problems inherent in the original novel and earlier film. It's focus on Cathy demonstrates how her unmotivated malice weakens the plot and how this full-scale portrait cruelly emphasizes Steinbeck's original adherence to the 1950s stereotype of a "bad" woman. In fact, the near pornographic production reveals a really unpleasant kinkiness in the whole conception, making it seem like Steinbeck's revenge on his divorced wives. In the final analysis, the eight-hour production only underscores the unwieldiness of the plot and theme, and the final incoherence of the whole story.

The final third, roughly the same material Kazan and Osborn used for the 1955 film, proves by far the best part of the television version. Director Harvey Hart, writer Richard Shapiro, and cinematographer Frank Stanley seem very much aware of Kazan's earlier film, often consciously imitating its literary and visual style. This visual replication only creates a feeling of dé jà vu, as the viewer is trapped in 1950s melodrama. Of course, this was exactly what Steinbeck originally wrote and Kazan filmed with James Dean, and just as it sold in 1952 and 1955, so it still sells today. Producer Rosenzweig's multi-million dollar gamble paid off with very high ratings, especially on Sunday and Wednesday, during the February "Sweeps Week." As the crow flies, it is not far from *East of Eden* to *Falcon's Crest* after all.

Among the three recent Steinbeck productions, Robert Blake's 1981 made-for-television film adaptation of *Of Mice and Men* stands out as a sincere and successful example of film artistry that in no way compromises Steinbeck's intentions. It's power derives as much or more from Milestone's

1939 film as from Steinbeck's novel, and it was fittingly
dedicated to the film director who had died in 1980. Perhaps
best known as television's colorful Detective Baretta, Blake
had been a child actor in Our Gang comedies and Red Ryder
Westerns until Milestone, his friend and mentor, gave him his
first adult role in a film about the Korean War, *Pork Chop Hill*
(1959). The stereotyped roles for which he is best known have
obscured his real talent as an actor, demonstrated in films
like *In Cold Blood* (1968) and *Tell Them Willie Boy Is Here*
(1969). In search of better parts, Blake became a producer;
with *Of Mice and Men* he mounted a splendid version of the
novel in which he superbly plays a George Milton who is
somewhat more pragmatic and believable than the lyric
Burgess Meredith creation in 1939.

An amazing work, the televised *Of Mice and Men* virtually replicates Milestone's film sequence by sequence, scene
by scene, shot by shot. Blake worked from Milestone's shooting script, and he uses even some of the same camera
positions and angles. The only immediately discernable differences are the color photography, a new musical score, and
the different cast.

All of the casting is brilliant. Randy Quaid plays Lennie
as a gentle giant, a big kid rather than Lon Chaney's sympathetic monster. Lew Ayres, the protagonist of Milestone's
classic *All Quiet on the Western Front* (1930), delivers a
stunning portrait of Candy, one free of the slight sentimentalizing Roman Bohen brought to the original film. Cassie
Yates is nearly as good as Curly's wife, a more human and
feminine Mae. Though Blake's wife, Rennee is quite good as
Aunt Clara—a role created from some remarks in the novel
and originally planned for the earlier film—the inclusion of
this character weakens the sense of loneliness and isolation.
The rest of the cast also proves solid: Ted Neely as Curly,
Mitchell Ryan as Slim, veteran Pat Hingle as Mr. Jackson,
Whitman Mayo as Crooks, Dennis Fimple as Whit, and Pat
Corley as Carlson.

The location shots and period recreations are flawlessly

captured in a muted color scheme by cinematographer Neil Roach; however, the photography does not quite achieve Milestone's stylized balance of realistic and expressionistic elements. Of course, director Reza Badiyi and television adaptor E. Nick Alexander have the help of the Milestone/ Solow script, but their cutting for television is intelligent. George Remoris's musical score—based mostly on traditional folk songs like "Red River Valley" and "Shenandoah"—is almost as good as Aaron Copland's original score. In all, it is the kind of production that occasionally justifies the existence of the television networks.

IX. CANNERY ROW

David S. Ward's *Cannery Row*, released in February 1982, is the most recent filmic adaptation of Steinbeck's fiction. This stylish, zippy production proved modestly successful with both the critics and the public, but the student of Steinbeck and film must wonder why it finally became a movie a generation after its publication. Like the television *East of Eden, Cannery Row* is most significant in revealing the flaws in the original fiction and in confirming the course of the author's decline after World War II.

   Cannery Row seemed destined for the movies from Steinbeck's first conception of it. He had been introduced to the denizens of Monterey's waterfront by his friend Ed Ricketts in the early 1930s, long before his literary success with his droll stories of Monterey's *paisanos* in *Tortilla Flat* (1935), and it seemed likely that he could someday use them as the focus of another popular success. At least his editor, Pascal Covici, thought so. After his harrowing experiences in World War II, Steinbeck finally began a book about the Row as a means of relaxing his tensions. Finished in little more than a few months; it was published in 1945—ironically just as the Row was being abandoned because the sardine beds had been fished out during the war.

A best seller despite critical disapproval, it was optioned by producer Berny Byrens in July 1945; however, no production ensued and after three years all rights reverted to Steinbeck, who discussed film possibilities with Lewis Milestone. Again nothing happened, until Frank Loesser contacted Steinbeck about a musical version of the novel in 1952.[4] Steinbeck's efforts to provide a plot for the nearly plotless book resulted in *Sweet Thursday* (1954), the sentimental sequel in which Doc finds true happiness with a kind-hearted hooker. Rodgers and Hammerstein finally did the stage musical—appropriately titled *Pipe Dream* (1955)—and they held the movie rights; but even after a season on Broadway, it did not make the screen. *Cannery Row* was clearly not the stuff of the 1960s, but in 1976 screenwriter David S. Ward interested producer Michael Phillips in the project. After three years of rejections, a package was finally put together at MGM in 1980.

Ward's persistence was repaid by a chance to direct his first film. It was not to be an easy production. He planned location shooting, but Monterey's once abandoned waterfront had become a row of trendy boutiques and restaurants (several named for Steinbeck or his characters). Rather than attempt to reconstitute Steinbeck's street, the production team created it from scratch on MGM's Stage 30, once the home of Freed Unit musicals like *Singing in the Rain* (1952). The tank in which Esther Williams once sported became the Pacific Ocean, and the most extensive interior-exterior set in a generation was created by British set designer Richard MacDonald. The cinematographer chosen was Swedish *emigré* Sven Nyquist, who had begun his career with director Ingmar Bergman. His touch was deft with studio scenes, and his location shots of the Pacific proved breathtaking. In other words, Steinbeck's *Cannery Row* was replicated, both outside and in, with loving care for detail.

One of the delays on the Ward/Phillips/MGM package was occasioned by the need to sign big name leads. Ward, who had written *The Sting* (1973), tried to interest Robert

Redford, but settled for Nick Nolte, who in turn attracted Raquel Welch. When, after shooting started, the erstwhile glamour girl stalked off Stage 30, she was replaced by a pretty and peppy newcomer, Debra Winger. (Ms. Welch, who claimed she was being exploited for her name, countered with a hefty lawsuit.) Other performers included Audra Lindley as Fauna, the platinum-hearted madam, and Frank McRae, M. Emmet Walsh, Sunshine Parker, and Santos Morales. The package was held together—more or less— by Jack Nitzche's score of 1940s pop tunes and John Huston's voice-over narration.

This considerable array of talent and an outlay of $11.3 million elicited a product which in 1981 proved popular with many of the critics outside New York, but not enough so with the public to win back its investments. The truth is *Cannery Row* is an ingratiating film that tries hard to please, but lacks the sparkle to make it a hit. It is also quite lacking in interest for the serious filmgoer or the serious student of John Steinbeck.

Richard MacDonald's remarkable set provides the controlling metaphor for the film; the "Cannery Row" we see is obviously unreal, a Fantasyland, a contemporary theme park rather than a revival of the old Hollywood. Everything looks "right," from Doc's specimans trucked in from Monterey to the wallpaper in the Bear Flag "Restaurant," the local hooker shop. But nothing *is* right; nothing is real or redolent of the sea, of fishing, of fighting, drinking, or whoring. It's all sanitized, made safe—and given a big fat happy ending—for a couple of pretty faces like Nolte and Winger.

Debra Winter herself has said of *Cannery Row* that it is "fairy tale." She's right, of course, but this fairy tale is closer to one from the Disney Studios than to the one by Brothers Grimm. And her part is the major fantasy element. Suzy is not just the typical Steinbeckian golden-hearted whore, but Cinderella, Snow White, and Sleeping Beauty all rolled into one. Her fairy godmother—Fauna—transforms her from a hooker into a "lady," and her brood of misfits facilitates the inevitable romance with Prince Charming. Although a young woman of considerable charm and talent—blessed with strong physical attributes, including a husky voice that recalls Lauren Bacall in the early Bogart films—she can do little to redeem lines that are excruciating in their banality.

Nick Nolte has a bit more to work with as Doc, a character based on Steinbeck's brilliant friend Ricketts. He and Winger do strike some emotional sparks in their first meeting, their first jitterbug dance (which becomes a comic wrestling match), and their first real date. Again, the critic can sense Nolte searching for somewhere to go with his character—somewhere other than the obligatory happy ending. In the final analysis, though Nolte shows the professionalism already evidenced in the TV mini-series based on Irwin Shaw's *Rich Man, Poor Man* (1977) or the movie based on Robert Stone's *Dog Soldiers* and renamed *Who'll Stop the Rain* (1978), Doc, the reluctant Prince Charming, has no real dramatic possibilities.

The rest of the cast labors hard to be funny and cute, and sometimes is. The "frog-gigging" scene and the first, disastrous party at Doc's evoke some genuine laughs, but the second party and the machinations in behalf of Suzy are merely cutesy. An occasional insight or image stands out—a phrase from Steinbeck in Huston's gravelly narration or one of Nyquist's exquisite images of the sea. Yet there are not enough of them.

The overall effect is corny. We are presented with fairy-tale characters, a daydream plot, a nostalgic set, and a warm-hearted theme. Though *Cannery Row* is occasionally an amusing film, it fails to meet even the level of adult entertainment Steinbeck created in his original novel. Like *Sweet Thursday* on which it is more firmly based, it is one more piece in the puzzle of John Steinbeck's artistic decline during the postwar period. Only in this sense does it provide a fitting conclusion to a discussion of John Steinbeck and film.

X. SOME CONCLUSIONS

The recent movie version of *Cannery Row*—begun almost four decades after the novel was first published—and the television versions of *East of Eden* and *Of Mice and Men* demonstrate that filmmakers and audiences continue to feel an affinity for Steinbeck's fiction. If he is one of our major writers most often chosen for adaptation, it is because the influence of film—for good and ill—is inherent in his work. When Steinbeck balanced his impulse toward romantic allegory with the documentary realism of the 1930s the result was strong, significant fiction. When he abandoned the realistic and documentary modes for a sentimental and meretricious imitation of the silver screen, film began to have an adverse and eventually fatal influence on his fiction.

After an apprentice period marked by the influence of nineteenth century romanticism and 1920s modernism, particularly as combined in the example of D. H. Lawrence, Steinbeck entered his major period of development with *In Dubious Battle* (1936). *Of Mice and Men* (1937), *The Long Valley* (1938), and *The Grapes of Wrath* (1939) followed, establishing Steinbeck as the spokesman for his time and securing him a permanent place in American literary culture. In the mood of the period, his writing balanced harsh realistic observation with human compassion. Essentially, Steinbeck drew this documentary impulse from the photography and films of the period, and it made his books especially adaptable for the movies. Lewis Milestone's *Of Mice and Men* (1939) and John Ford's *The Grapes of Wrath* (1940) are not only fine adaptations, they are among those Hollywood movies from the period that retain a sense of artistic honesty and emotional immediacy. Steinbeck's documentary, *The Forgotten Village* (1941), corroborates the realistic vision of his best work.

Steinbeck's long decline is paradoxically involved with increasing popular success. His works of the war years, both literary and filmic, proved propagandistic, nostalgic, or both. Of course, American film moved in the same directions, toward John Wayne's stoic heroics and Judy Garland's throat-catching sentimentality. As films, *The Moon Is Down* (1943) and *A Medal For Benny* (1945) are movies light years away from the realism and humanity of *Of Mice and Men* (1939) or *The Grapes of Wrath* (1940), and even collaboration with a major director, Alfred Hitchcock, on *Lifeboat* (1944) could not salvage that ill-fated allegory. With the publication of *Cannery Row* in 1945, Steinbeck inexorably turned toward easy past success in a reprise of *Tortilla Flat* (novel 1935, film 1942). From here on his work seemed inspired not by reality but the movie versions of his earlier books.

Perhaps a perfect example of this tendency in the post-war period is his own screenplay for *The Red Pony* (1949) which transforms his realistic initiation tale into a sentimental imitation of initiation. Of course, the major failure is the novel *East of Eden* (1952), Steinbeck's attempt at a California epic to stand with *The Grapes of Wrath*. Elia Kazan's film version (1955) somewhat improves this rambling family saga in its dramatic condensation, yet the film's fashionable 1950s psychology and symbolism derive directly from the book. The trite Hollywood version of *The Wayward Bus* (1957) similarly reveals the faults of the 1947 novel on which it was based.

The exceptions to this marked decline are two works about Mexico, both inspired by film. Steinbeck's short novel, *The Pearl* (1947) proves his most remarkable postwar fiction, a return to the balance of documentary and allegory in a perfect parable about the human condition. His screenplay for *Viva Zapata!* (1952) recalls not only *The Pearl* but the realism of *The Grapes of Wrath*. The contrasting filmic productions these works received do not destroy them as important indicators of Steinbeck's lost talents. In his final writings Steinbeck seemed to divide his once balanced modes of fantasy and documentary—fabrication in *The Short Reign of Pippin IV* (1957) and nonfiction in *Travels With Charley* (1962)—a development also corroborated in recent film and television adaptations.

Although he ultimately fell short of greatness, no doubt

exists that in his best work John Steinbeck achieved an important and permanent artistic vision. In his Nobel Prize speech of 1962, the writer indicated what he tried to accomplish in his work.

> The ancient commission of the writer has not changed. He is charged with exposing our many grievous faults and failures, with dredging up to the light our dark and dangerous dreams, for the purpose of improvement.
>
> Furthermore, the writer is delegated to declare and to celebrate man's proven capacity for greatness of heart and spirit—for gallantry in defeat, for courage, compassion, and love. In the endless war against weakness and despair, these are the bright rally-flags of hope and of emulation. I hold that a writer who does not passionately believe in the perfectibility of man has no dedication nor membership in literature.

No American writer has better exposed the dark underside of the American Dream nor better traced the lineaments of the American Nightmare—and few have so successfully celebrated the great hope which underlies the belief in human potential. Steinbeck's best fictions always picture a paradise lost, but they posit a future paradise to be regained. The light and shadows of the best films based on them replicate the complex emotions inherent in his words. Surely an artist has no more serious commission than the exposure of our dark dreams and the celebration of our bright potential.

Notes

Chapter One

1 Important works on the relationship of film and literature include: George Bluestone, *Novels into Film* (Berkeley: University of California, 1966); Keith Cohn, *Film and Fiction: The Dynamics of Exchange* (New Haven: Yale University Press, 1979); Claude-Edmonde Magny, *The Age of the American Novel: The Film Aesthetic of Fiction Between the Two Wars* (New York: Frederick Ungar, 1972); Edward Murray, *The Cinematic Imagination: Writers and the Motion Pictures* (New York: Frederick Ungar, 1972); Robert Richardson, *Literature and Film*, (Bloomington: Indiana University Press, 1969); Alan Spiegel, *Fiction and the Camera Eye: Visual Consciousness in Film and the Modern Novel*, (Charlottesville: University of Virginia, 1976).

2 Important considerations of Steinbeck and film include: Michael Burrows, *John Steinbeck and His Films*, (Cornwall: Primestyle, 1970); Warren French, *Filmguide to The Grapes of Wrath* (Bloomington: Indiana University Press, 1973); Magny, *op. cit*; Robert Morsberger, "Steinbeck's Screenplays and Productions," in *Viva Zapata!* (New York: Viking, 1975); Murray, *op. cit.* An important unpublished source is Davis Gary Corbett's Ph.D. Dissertation, *John Steinbeck in Films: An Analysis of Realism in the Novel and in Film—A Nonteleological Approach* (University of Southern California, 1975). Corbett's study is a full length, thorough consideration of Steinbeck's films. It contains many useful details and sound critical insights. In general, it comes to conclusions similar to this study. However, Corbett's study is weakened by a theoretical orientation which burdens his analysis with difficult definitions of "objective" and "subjective" realism. These general definitions in turn lead to some particular assertions which this study contradicts. For example, Corbett sees the

179

adaptation of *East of Eden* by Elia Kazan as the most important of the Steinbeck films, while this study finds it a tedious, pretentious work, only slightly more successful than Steinbeck's disastrous failure in the novel.

3 For a handy compilation of film adaptations of Modern American novels, See Gerald Peary and Roger Shatzkin, *The Modern American Novel and the Movies* (New York: Frederick Ungar, 1978), pp. 349–429. An excellent bibliography follows their filmography.

4 Critics of Steinbeck and film have mentioned the positive influence of the documentary tradition, particularly Peter Lisca in *The Wide World of John Steinbeck* (New Brunswick, New Jersey: Rutgers University Press, 1958). Many others have briefly considered the negative influence of Hollywood, particularly Magny and Murray in the works cited above. This study is the first to combine these observations and to support them with a full analysis of the Steinbeck films.

5 The best biography of Steinbeck is Thomas Kiernan's *The Intricate Music* (Boston: Little, Brown, 1979).

6 One of the best, short summaries of the 1930s is Malcom Cowley's in *And I Worked at the Writer's Trade* (New York: Viking, 1978), Chapter VII, "The 1930's: Faith and Works."

7 See Donald Worster, *Dust Bowl: The Southern Plains in the 1930's* (New York: Oxford, 1979), especially pages 32ff.

8 The most important general work on the documentary thrust of the decade is William Stott, *Documentary Expression in 1930's America* (New York: Oxford, 1973). His excellent bibliography points to other works on the various art forms and individual artists.

9 The date of Milestone's film is often given as 1940, reflecting the New York opening in January of that year. This writer prefers 1939 because the film was made and released that year, (December 22, 1939 in Hollywood). The earlier date more clearly indicates that the film was completed and released before the film version of *The Grapes of Wrath*.

Chapter Two

I. THE EARLY WORKS

1 Thomas Kiernan, *The Intricate Music: A Biography of John Steinbeck* pp. 16–19.

2 *Ibid.*, p. 119.

3 Nelson Valjean, *John Steinbeck: The Errant Knight* (San Francisco: Chronicle Books, 1975), p. 135.

4 Kiernan, pp. 159–163. Also see Richard Astro, *Steinbeck and Ricketts* (Minneapolis: University of Minnesota, 1973).

5 Arthur Kinney, "The Arthurian Cycle in *Tortilla Flat*," *Modern Fiction Studies*, Vol 9: 11–20.

6 Elaine Steinbeck and Robert Wallsten, eds., *Steinbeck: A Life in Letters*, (New York: Viking, 1975), p. 98.

7 *Ibid.*

II. OF MICE AND MEN

1 Charles Higham and Joel Greenberg, "Lewis Milestone," in *The Celluloid Muse: Hollywood Directors Speak*, (New York: Viking, 1972), p. 158. On the director's career also see Joseph R. Millichap, *Lewis Milestone* (Boston: Little, Brown, 1981).

2 Charles Shibuk, *An Index to the Films of Lewis Milestone*, (New York: Huff Memorial Film Society, 1958), p. 3.

3 Quentin Reynolds, "That's How Pictures Are Born. *Of Mice and Men*," *Colliers*, Vol. 105 (January 6, 1940), pp. 14–15.

4 *Ibid.*

5 *Ibid.*

6 *Ibid.*

7 William K. Everson, *The Films of Hal Roach* (New York: Museum of Modern Art, 1971), p. 77.

8 *John Steinbeck: A Life In Letters*, p. 195.

9 Pathfinder Edition of the novel, (New York, 1971), p. 2.

10 The picture is reproduced in *Years of Protest: A Collection of American Writings of the 1930's*, edited by Jack Salzman and Barry Wallenstein, (New York: Pegasus, 1967), p. 73.

11 William Everson comes to similar conclusions in "Thoughts on a Great Adaptation," in *The Modern American Novel and the Movies*, edited by Gerald Peary and Roger Shatzkin, (New York, Frederick Ungar, 1978), pp. 63–69.

III. THE GRAPES OF WRATH

1 Important considerations of *The Grapes of Wrath* as film include all of the works cited in Note 2 to Chapter One, as well as: George Bluestone, *Novels Into Film*, (Berkeley: University of California

Press, 1966); Janey Place, "*The Grapes of Wrath:* A Visual Analysis," *Film Comment* 12 (September–October, 1976), 46–51; Russell Campbell, "Tramping Out the Vintage: Sour Grapes" in *The Modern Novel and the Movies,* edited by Gerald Peary and Roger Shatzkin (New York: Frederick Ungar, 1978), pps. 107–118; Vivian C. Sobchack, "*The Grapes of Wrath* (1940): Thematic Emphasis Through Visual Style," *American Quarterly* 31 (Winter, 1979), 596–615.

2 The best study of this documentary thrust is William Stott, *Documentary Expression and 1930's America,* (New York: Oxford, 1973). Stott's thorough, penetrating analysis of the decade's culture is a major contribution in American studies.

3 *Agee on Film, Vol. I* (New York: McDowell, Obolensky, 1958), pp. 296–297.

4 Kiernan, p. 228.

5 Stott, p. 122.

6 Kiernan, p. 216.

7 Jackson J. Benson, " 'To Tom Who Lived It': John Steinbeck and Its Man from Weedpatch," *Journal of Modern Literature* 5 (April, 1976), 151–194.

8 F. Jack Hurley, *Portrait of A Decade* (Baton Rouge: Louisiana State University Press, 1927), p. 140. Milton Meltzer, *Dorothea Lange* (New York: Farrar, Strauss, Giroux, 1978), pp. 202–203.

9 John Grierson's definition is quoted in Thomas Bohn, *An Historical and Descriptive Analysis of the Why We Fight Series* (New York: Arno, 1977), p. 10.

10 Several Hogue paintings were reproduced in *Life,* June 21, 1937, 60–61.

11 Despite the deficiencies of the Ford version, try to imagine *The Grapes of Wrath* as directed by Frank Capra, Howard Hawks, or William Wyler.

12 Peter Bogdanovich, *John Ford* (Berkeley: University of California Press, 1968), p. 72. The best study of Ford is Andrew Sarris, *The John Ford Movie Mystery* (Bloomington: Indiana University Press, 1975).

13 Page references to the Viking Critical Edition of the novel, edited by Peter Lisca, (New York: Viking, 1972), will be given in the text in parentheses.

14 "A Family in a Ford," *Film Comment* 12 (September–October, 1976), 46.

15 Quotations from the film are taken from the final print, which often differs from the screenplay. The screenplay is contained in *Twenty Best Film Plays*, edited by John Gassner and Dudley Nichols (New York: Crown, 1943), pp. 333–377.

16 The depiction of crops destroyed recalls the conclusion of Dutch documentarian Joris Ivens's influential *The New Earth* (1934); Ivens later worked with Pare Lorentz for the U.S. Film Service.

17 In the novel Tom and Ma part in a dark cave where he must hide like a hunted animal. Like Steinbeck's Mexican protagonists in "Flight," *The Pearl*, and *Viva Zapata!*, it seems Tom must be reduced to an animal level to achieve his full humanity and manhood.

IV. THE FORGOTTEN VILLAGE

1 Page references are to the Bantam Paperback Edition of 1961, the most readily available edition.

2 After World War II, Kline's career paralleled Steinbeck's, as he turned from documentaries to Hollywood potboilers with titles like *The Kid From Cleveland* (1951) and *Prince of Pirates* (1953).

3 Steinbeck evidently wrote the screenplay, which Kline says was very good. See the director's reminiscence piece, "On John Steinbeck," *Steinbeck Quarterly* 4 (Summer, 1971), 80–88.

4 The first choice of music director was Mexico's composer Silvestre Revueltas, who died as the film was being shot. Spencer Tracy was the first choice for narrator, but MGM kept him from participating in the project. Burgess Meredith, George in *Of Mice and Men*, did the narration. Finally it took the intervention of Eleanor Roosevelt to get the New York Review Board to allow the childbirth scenes to be screened.

5 Kline, *op. cit.*, 87.

6 John Steinbeck, *The Forgotten Village* (New York: Viking, 1941), p. 6.

7 Astro, p. 57.

8 Corbett, p. 89.

Chapter Three

I. A NEW DECADE

1 Valjean, p. 175–176.

2 Kiernan, p. 286.

3 Kiernan, p. 206.

4 Kline, p. 81.

5 Kiernan, p. 255

6 Corbett, p. 99.

7 Corbett, p. 103.

8 *Bombs Away: The Story of a Bomber Team.* (New York: Viking, 1942), p. 194.

9 John Ditsky develops at more length the contradiction and ironies of the book in "Steinbeck's *Bombs Away:* The Group Man in the Wild Blue Yonder," *Steinbeck Quarterly* 12 (Winter–Spring 1979), 5–14.

II. TORTILLA FLAT

1 Howard Levant comes to somewhat similar conclusions in *The Novels of John Steinbeck: A Critical Study* (Columbia: University of Missouri Press, 1974), pp. 69–73. Levant also puts emphasis on Steinbeck's later publication of allegorically structured novels, *East of Eden,* for example.

2 Valjean, pp. 136–137, 147.

3 *A Life in Letters,* p. 97.

4 On the Arthurian parallels see Arthur Kinney, *op. cit.;* and the essays on *Steinbeck and the Arthurian Tales,* edited by Tetsumaro Hayashi, (Muncie, Indiana: Ball State University: Steinbeck Monograph Series No. 5, 1975). Warren French remarks in *John Steinbeck* (Boston: G. K. Hall, 1975), p. 71, that Steinbeck may be spoofing Malory, a reasonable suggestion.

5 *A Life In Letters,* p. 111.

6 "My Short Novels," *Wings* (October, 1955), 6.

7 A play version stands between the novel and the film, as with *Of Mice and Men.* Jack Kirkland, best known for his dramatic version of *Tobacco Road* (1933) (filmed by John Ford in 1941) put Steinbeck's work on the stage in a sleazy production which lasted only four days on Broadway in 1938. Evidently, the play bore little relation to either the novel or the film, though it did have a happy ending.

8 Modern Library Edition (New York: Random House, 1937).

9 *Newsweek,* Vol. 19 (June 1, 1942), 66. The review in *Time,* Vol. 39 (May 18, 1942), 84, says that Steinbeck tried to buy the film back from the studio for $10,000. This assertion is not supported by any

evidence, and it seems unlikely that the perennially strapped author would offer that much money to preserve a seven-year-old novel from Hollywood's sentimentalizing.

III. THE MOON IS DOWN

1 Kiernan, p. 258.
2 *Ibid.*
3 "My Short Novels," *Wings* (October, 1953), 6.
4 *The Moon Is Down* (New York: Viking, 1942), p. 186.
5 "Brighter Moon," *Newsweek*, Vol. 21 (April 5, 1943), 86.
6 *A Life In Letters*, p. 244.
7 "Brighter Moon," *Newsweek*, Vol. 21 (April 5, 1943), 86.
8 Bosley Crowther, *New York Times* (March 27, 1943), 8.
9 Vol. 156 (May 1, 1943), 643.
10 *New York Times* (March 27, 1943), 8.
11 *New York Times* (January 14, 1943), 25.

IV. LIFEBOAT

1 *A Life In Letters*, p. 249.
2 *Ibid.*
3 *Ibid.*
4 Unpublished typescript, *Lifeboat*, by John Steinbeck (Revised) March 26, 1943. (The writer wishes to thank Prof. Robert Morsberger for providing a copy of the work.)
5 In his dissertation, Corbett quotes Steinbeck's agent to the effect that the writer worked from an existing studio property. This seems unlikely from the letter cited above in which Steinbeck provides a detailed description of writing the story treatment and does not mention working from an existing property. See Corbett, p. 107.
6 François Truffaut, *Hitchcock* (New York: Simon and Schuster, 1967) p. 113.
7 The casting of William Bendix as Gus also creates a problem for audience now conditioned to the actor's personna of Chester Riley, the amiable working stiff of the popular *The Life of Riley* radio program. Although Bendix's performance, like Bankhead's, may be a career best, moviegoers tended to anticipate Gus's reaction to tragedy with Riley's stock line: "What a revoltin' development this is!" Bendix played Riley not only in the movie,

The Life of Riley (1947), but on the radio from 1944–1951, and on television from 1953 to 1958. The program was always amusing, and notable as one of the few radio or television series to have a working class protagonist.

8 Truffaut, p. 113.

9 *Ibid.*

10 Hitchcock had difficulty making his usual cameo appearance in the tight confines of the lifeboat; he solved the problem by having one of the survivors read an old newspaper showing an ad for "Reduco," a diet pill. Hitchcock, who had recently lost a good deal of weight, was featured in the before and after pictures. Later, he received inquiries about where to buy the product. See John Russell Taylor, *Hitch* (Boston: Faber, 1973), pp. 190–191.

11 *A Life in Letters.*

12 *Ibid.*

13 *Ibid.*

14 For differing views see: Steven J. Federle, "*Lifeboat* as Allegory: Steinbeck and the Demon of War," *Steinbeck Quarterly* 12 (Winter/Spring 1977), 14–20, and Robert E. Morsberger, "Adrift in Steinbeck's *Lifeboat*" *Film/Literature Quarterly* 4 (Fall, 1976) 325–338.

V. A MEDAL FOR BENNY

1 It is not clear if *Lifeboat* or *A Medal For Benny* was written first. Corbett in his dissertation claims *Lifeboat* followed *A Medal For Benny*, but he doesn't explain the production lag which occurred. In the absence of strong evidence this study considers the films in the order of their production. See Corbett, p. 104.

2 Corbett, p. 104.

3 See John Gassner and Dudley Nicholls, *Best Film Plays of 1945*, (New York, 1945).

4 Corbett, p. 105.

5 May 24, 1945, 15.

6 Volume 42, 119 (May 18, 1945).

7 *Agee On Film*, p. 169.

8 Volume 21, June 2, 1945, 64.

VI. THE WAR AND AFTER

1 Kiernan, p. 264.

2 *Ibid.* p. 267.

3 In this regard, it seems ironic that his son, John Steinbeck IV.,

wrote one of the best books—*In Touch* (New York: Knopf, 1969)—about the Vietnam War.

4 Kiernan, p. 267.
5 See Corbett, pp. 114–115.
6 *A Life In Letters*, p. 269, and Kiernan, p. 323.
7 Kiernan, pp. 268–278.

Chapter Four

I. AFTER THE WAR

1 Valjean, pp. 22–23, 80–81.
2 Kiernan, p. 269.
3 *The Pearl* (New York: Viking, 1947). All page references are to this edition.

II. THE PEARL

1 Lisca, p. 218.
2 Corbett, p. 122.
3 *The Log From the Sea of Cortez*, p. 102.
4 Several critics suggest the medieval allegory, *Pearl* as a source of this work. Steinbeck was well read in medieval literature, and the correspondences between the works prove interesting, but not conclusive.
5 It is unfortunate that the filmmakers were not inspired by the powerful illustrations done for the book by Mexican muralist José Clemente Orozco.
6 "The Film Version of Steinbeck's *The Pearl*," *Steinbeck Quarterly*, 4: 88–92.

III. THE RED PONY

1 Kiernan, p. 277
2 Kiernan, p. 279
3 Kiernan, p. 279–280
4 Kiernan, p. 280
5 Steinbeck also discussed the project with Victor Fleming and Spencer Tracy. See: *A Life in Letters*, 195–196, and Kiernan, p. 246.
6 Lisca, p. 93
7 Perhaps because of the use of the name Jody in Marjorie Kinnan Rawlings's *The Yearling* (1947), a very similar story.

8 Peter Miles, brother of Gigi, Gerald, and Janine Perreau, appeared in eight films between 1947 and 1951, none of any importance other than *The Red Pony*.

9 *The Red Pony, A Cutting Continuity* (Republic Studios, 1949.) p. 1. The screenplay has not been published.

10 Ibid, p. 40

11 Also see Joseph R. Millichap, *Lewis Milestone*, pp. 141–142, 157–158.

IV. VIVA ZAPATA!

1 Kiernan, p. 277.

2 According to Elia Kazan the film was actually his idea, one he had as early as 1935. (See Michel Ciment, *Kazan on Kazan* New York: Viking, 1974, p. 88.) In "An American Cold Warrior: *Viva Zapata!* (1952)." Paul J. Underwood traces Hollywood's interest in Zapata back to *Viva Villa!* (1933) and implies that 20th Century-Fox assigned Kazan and Steinbeck to a work already in preparation. (See John E. O'Connor and Martin A. Jackson, *American History/ American Film: Interpreting the Hollywood Image* [New York: Frederick Ungar, 1979], p. 188.) Since neither of these accounts develop Steinbeck's connection with the abortive Mexican production, or consider his screenplay closely, they seem to slight his role in creating the Zapata film. The analysis which follows will show that the final product is quite typical of Steinbeck's work, indicating the writer's central role in the evolution of the film.

3 Kiernan, pp. 289–290.

4 Kiernan, p. 293.

5 Underwood, p. 196.

6 The definitive work in English on Zapata is John Womack, Jr., *Zapata and the Mexican Revolution.* (New York: Knopf, 1969).

7 See Underwood, *op. cit.*, and Peter Biskind, "Ripping Off Zapata's Revolution Hollywood Style," *Cineaste* 7 (#2), 10–15.

8 Unless otherwise indicated quotations are from *Viva Zapata! The Original Screenplay by John Steinbeck*, edited by Robert Morsberger, (New York: Viking, 1975). Numbers in parentheses indicate page numbers of that publication.

9 Morsberger, ed., *Viva Zapata!* p. 137.

10 *Ibid.*, p. 138.

11 *Kazan on Kazan*, p. 89.

12 *Kazan on Kazan*, pp. 97–98. Kazan credits Zanuck with Zapata's

white horse, though the animal is featured in Steinbeck's screenplay.

13 *Kazan on Kazan*, p. 92.

14 *Ibid.*

15 *Kazan on Kazan*, p. 99. (Eisenstein's Mexican film seems to have had an unfortunate influence on both *The Forgotten Village* and *The Pearl.*)

16 *Kazan on Kazan*, p. 91.

17 *Ibid.*

V. EAST OF EDEN

1 Kiernan, p. 297.

2 *Journal of a Novel: The East of Eden Letters* (New York: Viking, 1969), p. 180.

3 *Ibid*, pp. 179–182.

4 Corbett, p. 193.

5 In his *East of Eden Letters*, Steinbeck admits that he doesn't understand Adam's motivation in marrying Cathy; see p. 39.

6 *Kazan on Kazan* p. 123.

7 *Ibid.*, p. 122–123.

8 *Library Journal* 80:555.

9 *Nation* 180:294.

10 *Commonweal* 61:604.

11 John Steinbeck, "An Appreciation," *East of Eden Premiere Program* (Warner Brothers, 1955), not paginated.

12 *Ibid.*

13 See Raymond Massey, *When I Was Young* (Boston: Little, Brown, 1976).

VI. THE WAYWARD BUS

1 Kiernan, pp. 300–301.

2 *A Life In Letters*, pp. 450–453, 456–457.

3 Kiernan, p. 301.

4 *Sweet Thursday*, (New York: Viking, 1954).

5 Quoted by Kiernan, p. 281.

6 *The Wayward Bus* (New York: Viking, 1947).

7 *A Life In Letters*, p. 284.

VII. FLIGHT AND FINAL WORKS

1 Steinbeck had made one other screen appearance in a similar narrator's role for *O. Henry's Full House*, a 1952 anthology film of

five O. Henry stories done by five directors, released by 20th Century-Fox.

2 Robert E. Morsberger, "Steinbeck on Screen," in Tetsumaro Hayashi, ed., *A Study Guide to Steinbeck* (Metuchen, N.J.: Scarecrow, 1974) p. 287.

3 *Ibid.*

4 *Ibid.*

VIII. TELEVISION

1 Corbett, p. 223.

2 At this time CBS News also produced a program entitled "The Great American Novel: *The Grapes of Wrath.*" Richard Boone read bits of Steinbeck's novel, while documentary films of contemporary migrant workers were shown. The two elements do not cohere.

3 For a differing view, see Corbett pp. 133–135.

Selected Bibliography

I. Works by John Steinbeck

FICTION

Cup of Gold. New York: Robert M. McBride & Co., 1929.

The Pastures of Heaven. New York: Brewer, Warren & Putnam, 1932.

To a God Unknown. New York: Robert O. Ballou, 1933.

Tortilla Flat. New York: Covici-Friede, 1935.

In Dubious Battle, New York: Covici-Friede, 1936.

The Red Pony. New York: Covici-Friede, 1937; The Viking Press, 1945. (Included in *The Long Valley,* 1938).

Of Mice and Men. New York: Covici-Friede, 1937.

The Long Valley. New York: The Viking Press, 1938

The Grapes of Wrath. New York: The Viking Press, 1939.

The Moon Is Down. New York: The Viking Press, 1942.

Cannery Row. New York: The Viking Press, 1945.

The Wayward Bus. New York: The Viking Press, 1947.

The Pearl. New York: The Viking Press, 1947.

Burning Bright. New York: The Viking Press, 1950.

East of Eden. New York: The Viking Press, 1952.

Sweet Thursday. New York: The Viking Press, 1954.

The Short Reign of Pippin IV: A Fabrication. New York: The Viking Press, 1957.

The Winter of Our Discontent. New York: The Viking Press, 1961.

The Acts of King Arthur and His Noble Knights. Edited by Chase Horton. New York: Farrar, Straus, Giroux, 1976.

NONFICTION

Their Blood Is Strong (pamphlet). San Francisco: Simon J. Lubin Society of California, Inc., 1938. [Articles published in *San Francisco News,* October 5–12, 1936, as "The Harvest Gypsies."]

Sea of Cortez: A Leisurely Journal of Travel and Research (in collaboration with Edward F. Ricketts). New York: The Viking Press, 1941.

Bombs Away: The Story of a Bomber Team. New York: The Viking Press, 1942.

A Russian Journal (with pictures by Robert Capa). New York: The Viking Press, 1948.

The Log from the Sea of Cortez. New York: The Viking Press, 1951. [The narrative portion of *Sea of Cortez* and a tribute, "About Ed Ricketts."]

Once There Was a War. New York: The Viking Press, 1958. [Steinbeck's wartime dispatches published in the *New York Herald Tribune,* June–December, 1943.]

Travels with Charley in Search of America. New York: The Viking Press, 1962.

America and Americans. New York: The Viking Press, 1966.

Journal of a Novel: The East of Eden Letters. New York: The Viking Press, 1969.

Steinbeck: A Life in Letters. Edited by Elaine Steinbeck and Robert Wallsten. New York: The Viking Press, 1975.

PLAYS

Of Mice and Men. New York: Covici-Friede, 1937.

The Moon Is Down. New York: The Viking Press, 1943.

Burning Bright. New York: Dramatists Play Service, 1951.

Pipe Dream (musical comedy by Richard Rodgers and Oscar Hammerstein II based on *Sweet Thursday*). New York: The Viking Press, 1956.

FILM STORIES AND SCREENPLAYS

The Forgotten Village (documentary). Herbert Kline, Producer, 1941. Story and script. New York: The Viking Press, 1941.

Lifeboat. 20th Century-Fox Film Corp., 1944. Story. Unpublished.

A Medal for Benny. Paramount Studios, 1945. Story, with Jack Wagner. *Best Film Plays*—1945, ed. by John Gassner and Dudley Nichols. New York: Crown, 1946.

The Pearl (from his novel). RKO, 1947. Script. Unpublished.

The Red Pony (from his stories). Feldman Group Productions and Lewis Milestone Productions, 1949. Script. Unpublished.

Viva Zapata. 20th Century-Fox Film Corp., 1952. Story and script.

The Original Screenplay by John Steinbeck, edited by Robert E. Morsberger. New York: The Viking Press, 1975.

II. Secondary Sources

Astro, Richard. *Steinbeck and Ricketts.* Minneapolis: University of Minnesota Press, 1973.

Bluestone, George. *Novels Into Film.* Berkeley: University of California Press, 1966.

Burrows, Michael. *John Steinbeck and His Films.* Cornwall: Primestyle, 1970.

Cohn, Keith. *Film and Fiction: The Dynamics of Exchange.* New Haven: Yale University Press, 1979.

Corbett, Davis Gary. *John Steinbeck in Films: An Analysis of Realism in the Novel and in the Film—A Nonteleological Approach.* Doctoral Dissertation: University of Southern California, 1975.

French, Warren. *Filmguide to the Grapes of Wrath.* Bloomington: Indiana University Press, 1973.

————. *John Steinbeck.* Boston, G. K. Hall, 1975.

Hayashi, Tetsumaro. *A Study Guide to Steinbeck.* Metuchen, New Jersey: Scarecrow Press, 1974.

Kiernan, Thomas. *The Intricate Music: A Biography of John Steinbeck.* Boston: Little, Brown, 1979.

Levant, Howard. *The Novels of John Steinbeck: A Critical Study.* Columbia: University of Missouri Press, 1974.

Lisca, Peter, editor. *The Grapes of Wrath: Text and Criticism.* New York: The Viking Press, 1972.

————. *The Wide World of John Steinbeck.* New Brunswick, New Jersey: Rutgers University Press, 1958.

McCarthy, John. *John Steinbeck.* New York: Frederick Ungar, 1980.

Magny, Claude-Edmonde. *The Age of the American Novel: The Film Aesthetic of Fiction Between the Two Wars.* New York: Frederick Ungar, 1972.

Morsberger, Robert E., editor. *Viva Zapata: The Original Screenplay by John Steinbeck.* New York: The Viking Press, 1975.

Murray, Edward. *The Cinematic Imagination: Writers and the Motion Pictures.* New York: Frederick Ungar, 1972.

O'Connor, John E. and Jackson, Martin A., editors. *American History/American Film: Interpreting the Hollywood Image.* New York: Frederick Ungar, 1979.

Peary, Gerald and Shatzkin, Roger, editors. *The Modern American Novel and the Movies*. New York: Frederick Ungar, 1978.

Richardson, Robert. *Literature and Film*. Bloomington: University of Indiana Press, 1969.

Steinbeck, Elaine and Wallsten, Robert, editors. *Steinbeck: A Life In Letters*. New York: The Viking Press, 1975.

Spiegel, Alan. *Fiction and the Camera Eye: Visual Consciousness in Film and the Modern Novel*, Charlottesville: University of Virginia, 1976.

Stott, William. *Documentary Expression in 1930's America*. New York: Oxford Press, 1973.

Tedlock, E. W., Jr. and Wicker, C. V., editors. *Steinbeck and His Critics*. Albuquerque: University of New Mexico Press, 1957.

Valjean, Nelson. *John Steinbeck: The Errant Knight*. San Francisco: Chronicle Books, 1975.

Filmography

Of Mice and Men (1939)

Screenplay by Eugene Solow, adapted from the John Steinbeck novel and play.
Directed and produced by Lewis Milestone
Musical score by Aaron Copland
Photography by Norbert Brodine
A Hal Roach presentation
United Artists

CAST

George: Burgess Meredith
Lennie: Lon Chaney, Jr.
Mae: Betty Field
Slim: Charles Bickford
Curley: Bob Steel

Candy: Roman Bohnen
Whit: Noah Beery, Jr.
Jackson: Oscar O'Shea
Carlson: Granville Bates
Crooks: Leigh Whipper

The Grapes of Wrath (1940)

Screenplay by Nunnally Johnson, adapted from the novel by John Steinbeck.
Musical score by Alfred Newman
Directed by John Ford
Photography by Gregg Toland
Produced by Darryl F. Zanuck
Twentieth Century-Fox

CAST

Tom Joad: Henry Fonda
Ma Joad: Jane Darwell
Casy: John Carradine
Grampa: Charley Grapewin
Rosasharn: Dorris Bowdon
Pa Joad: Russell Simpson
Camp Director: Grant Mitchell

Al: O. Z. Whitehead
Muley: John Qualen
Noah: Frank Sully
Uncle John: Frank Darien
Winfield: Darryl Hickman
Ruthie Joad: Shirley Mills
Policeman: Ward Bond

The Forgotten Village (1941)

Story and screenplay be John Steinbeck
Music by Hanns Eisler
Photography by Alexander Hackensmid
Narrated by Burgess Meredith
Produced and directed by Herbert Kline
An Arthur Mayer-Joseph Burstyn release

CAST
The people of Santiago Pueblo.

Tortilla Flat (1942)

Screenplay by John Lee Mahin and Benjamin Glazer, based on the
    novel by John Steinbeck
Directed by Victor Fleming
Produced by Sam Zimbalist
MGM

CAST
Pilon: Spencer Tracy
Danny: John Garfield
Dolores (Sweets) Ramirez: Hedy Lamarr
Pablo: Akim Tamiroff
The Pirate: Frank Morgan
Jose Marie Corcoran: John Qualen
Tito Ralph: Sheldon Leonard
Portagee Joe: Allen Jenkins

The Moon Is Down (1943)

Screenplay by Nunnally Johnson, based on the novel by John
    Steinbeck
Directed by Irving Pichel
Photography by Arthur Miller
Produced by Nunnally Johnson
Twentiety Century-Fox

CAST
Colonel Lanser: Sir Cedric Hardwicke
Mayor Orden: Henry Travers
Dr. Winter: Lee J. Cobb
Molly Morden: Dorris Bowdon
Madame Orden: Margaret Wycherly
Lt. Tonder: Peter VanEyck
Peder: Irving Pichel
George Corell: E.J. Ballantine

Lifeboat (1944)

Screenplay by Jo Swerling, from a story by John Steinbeck
Directed by Alfred Hitchcock
Produced by Kenneth Macgowan
Twentieth Century-Fox

CAST

Connie Porter: Tallulah Bankhead
Gus: William Bendix
Willy: Walter Slezak
Alice Mackenzie: Mary Anderson
Rittenhouse: Henry Hull

Kovac: John Hodiak
Stanley Garrett: Hume Cronyn
Joe: Canada Lee
Mrs. Higgins: Heather Angel

A Medal for Benny (1945)

Screenplay by Frank Butler, from a story by John Steinbeck and
    Jack Wagner
Directed by Irving Pichel
Produced by Paul Jones
Paramount

CAST

Lolita Sierra: Dorothy Lamour
Joe Morales: Arturo De Cordova
Mayor: Grant Mitchell

Charley Martini: J. Carrol Naish
Raphael Catalina: Mikhail
Rasummy

The Pearl (1947)

Screenplay by John Steinbeck, Emilio Fernandez, and Jack Wagner
Directed by Emilio Fernandez
Photography by Gabrial Figuroa
Produced by Oscar Danugers
RKO

CAST

Kino: Pedro Armendariz
Juan: Maria Elena Marques

Broker: Fernando Wagner

The Red Pony (1949)

Screenplay by John Steinbeck
Music by Aaron Copland

Photography by Tony Gaudio
Directed and produced by Lewis Milestone
Republic

CAST

Alice Tiflin: Myrna Loy
Billy Buck: Louis Calhern
Fred Tiflin: Shepperd Strudwick

Tom [Jody]: Peter Miles
Teacher: Margaret Hamilton
Beau: Beau Bridges

Viva Zapata! (1952)

Screenplay by John Steinbeck
Directed by Elia Kazan
Photography by Joe MacDonald
Music by Alfred Newman
Produced by Darryl F. Zanuck
Twentieth Century-Fox

CAST

Emiliano Zapata: Marlon
Brando
Josefa: Jean Peters
Eufemio: Anthony Quinn
Fernando: Joseph Wiseman
Don Nacio: Arnold Moss
Soldadera: Margo

Pancho Villa: Alan Reed
Madero: Harold Gordon
Pablo: Lou Gilbert
Señora Espejo: Mildren Dun-
nock
Huerta: Frank Silvera
Diaz: Faye Roope

East of Eden (1955)

Screenplay by Paul Osborn, based on the novel by John Steinbeck
Music by Victor Young
Directed by Elia Kazan
Photography by Ted McCord
Warners

CAST

Abra: Julie Harris
Cal Trask: James Dean
Adam Trask: Raymond Massey
Aron Trask: Richard Davalos
Kate: Jo Van Fleet

Mr. Albrecht: Harold Gordon
Sam: Burl Ives
Will: Albert Dekker
Ann: Lois Smith
Joe: Timothy Carey

The Wayward Bus (1957)

Screenplay by Ivan Moffat, based on the novel by John Steinbeck
Directed by Victor Vicas
Produced by Charles Brackett
Twentieth Century-Fox

CAST

Johnny Chicoy: Rick Jason
Alice Chicoy: Joan Collins
Camille: Jayne Mansfield
Ernest Horton: Dan Dailey
Norma: Betty Lou Keim

Mildred Pritchard: Dolores
Michaels
Pritchard: Larry Keating
Morse: Robert Bray
Mrs. Pritchard: Kathryn Givney

Flight (1961)

Screenplay by Barnaby Conrad, adapted from the short story by
   John Steinbeck
Produced by Barnaby Conrad
Music written and played by Laurindo Almeida
Photography by Verne Carlson
Directed by Louis Bispo.

CAST

Narrator: John Steinbeck
Pepe: Efrain Ramirez
Mrs. Torres: Amelia Cortez

Emilio: Andrew Cortez
Rosa: Maria Gonzales

Cannery Row (1982)

Screenplay by David S. Ward, based on Steinbeck's novel and on his
   Sweet Thursday
Directed by David S. Ward
Produced by Michael Phillips
MGM
Set design by Richard MacDonald
Photography By Sven Nyquist
Music by Jack Nitzche

CAST

Doc: Nick Nolte
Suzy: Debra Winger
Fauna: Audra Lindley

Mac: M. Emmet Walsh
Hazel: Frank McRae

Index